D1194097

NATIONAL
GALLERY
LONDON

GREAT MUSEUMS OF THE WORLD

NATIONAL GALLERY LONDON

Paul Hamlyn LONDON · NEW YORK · SYDNEY · TORONTO

GREAT MUSEUMS OF THE WORLD

Editorial Director: Carlo Ludovico Ragghianti
Assistant: Giuliana Nannicini
Translation and Editing: Editors of Art News

Texts of this volume by Gigetta Dalli Regoli,
Giampaolo Gandolfo, Gian Lorenzo Mellini,
Raffaele Monti, Anna Pallucchini,
Rodolfo Pallucchini, Licia Ragghianti Collobi
Design by Fiorenzo Giorgi

Originally published in Italian by
Arnoldo Mondadori Editore, Milan
© 1969 Arnoldo Mondadori Editore–CEAM–Milan
© 1969 Photographs copyright by Kodansha Ltd.–Tokyo
This edition copyright © 1970 the Hamlyn Publishing Group Limited,
Feltham, Middlesex, England
All rights reserved
Printed and bound by Officine Grafiche Arnoldo Mondadori, Verona
ISBN 0 600 79313 3

INTRODUCTION

MICHAEL LEVEY
Keeper

Founded in 1824, the National Gallery is one of the youngest picture galleries of Europe. Unlike most other great European galleries, its nucleus was not a royal or princely collection taken over by the state. In England, the National Gallery is truly national, while the Royal Collection remains a separate entity, the private property of the reigning monarch.

The circumstances under which the National Gallery began are important for an understanding of its particular character and the course of its growth. It has never aimed to be a vast collection of paintings; today the collection numbers only about two thousand pictures — less than half the number in the Louvre, for example.

The Gallery was created on April 2, 1824. At the instigation of the Prime Minister, Lord Liverpool, Parliament voted £60,000 for the purchase, preservation and exhibition of the Angerstein collection, a group of thirty-eight paintings owned by John Julius Angerstein, a rich merchant who had died in 1823. Rumors that the Angerstein collection would be sold out of England had created a furor of protests. King George IV himself was reported to have advised the purchase of the collection.

On May 10, 1824, the National Gallery, then accommodated in Angerstein's London house, opened for the first time. The occasion does not seem to have created very great interest. Few people could have foreseen that within twenty years of its foundation the Gallery would contain such unique masterpieces as Jan van Eyck's *The Marriage of Giovanni Arnolfini and Giovanna Cenami* and Bellini's *The Doge Leonardo Loredan* — today among the most famous paintings in the world.

Although the Angerstein collection contained some important English pictures (among them Hogarth's series, *Marriage à la Mode*), English art has rarely been the dominant interest of English collectors in any period. The glories of Angerstein's collection lay elsewhere: in paintings by Rembrandt, Rubens, van Dyck and — above all —in a magnificent group of pictures by Claude Lorrain. There was also a miscellaneous assortment of Italian pictures, of which the most remarkable was the huge *The Resurrection of Lazarus* by Sebastiano del Piombo. Recently, this major example of High Renaissance art, executed at Rome in virtual competition with Raphael's *Transfiguration,* has been cleaned and restored; it had been half-concealed under heavily discolored varnish.

English taste has always responded to the Italian Renaissance and to the great achievements of seventeenth-century French painting, recognizing the superiority of most foreign schools of painting over the native English one. The Gallery has reflected this attitude from the first, and as a consequence has become one of the most balanced, probably *the* most balanced, of all European galleries. Because it is not based on the rich inheritance of a royal collection, the Gallery has had to acquire paintings. It has operated on the principle that it is a gallery of *art* — not a mere collection of historical objects. One masterpiece is worth more in aesthetic significance than twenty minor pictures, all with some historical interest.

In the early years of the National Gallery, it was most fortunate that several distinguished private collectors gave or bequeathed treasures from their collections to the new institution. Of these benefactors, Sir George Beaumont is individually the most outstanding, because he had urged the foundation of a national collection, had been a generous lender of his pictures to public exhibitions in London, and was himself a painter as well as a patron of Constable's. He owned the superb, panoramic Rubens' *Castle of Steen,* a picture that exudes an autumnal mellowness and serenity that seem to accord with the painter's own feelings late in life. Scarcely less personal and no less superb was Beaumont's single Canaletto, *The Stonemason's Yard.* A townscape, this picture conveys the poetry inherent in ordinary houses, a stretch of water and atmospheric sky. It is a personal view of Venice, probably painted for a resident there rather than a tourist. Although the Gallery has acquired several other fine Canaletto paintings, none equals the power of this masterpiece. Beaumont's genuine feeling for his pictures, and the effort it cost him to part with them, is revealed by the fact that he asked to retain for his lifetime a small but very beautiful Claude; it entered the Gallery only after his death in 1828.

In 1831, another benefactor, the Rev. William Holwell Carr, bequeathed his collection to the Gallery. This famous collection contained a number of remarkable pictures (including Rembrandt's *A Woman Bathing in a Stream*), and showed a marked sympathy for "painterly" works, glowing with color. The most outstanding picture in the Holwell Carr bequest was Tintoretto's *St. George and the Dragon,* which is still the Gallery's best work by a painter whose reputation was long overshadowed by Titian. In 1831 Tintoretto was not among the great or familiar names in the history of art. When the *St. George* was cleaned recently, Holwell Carr's perceptive taste was fully confirmed. Although on a small scale by Tintoretto's standards, this picture has all of his typical dynamism and brilliance; in fact, the smallness of the canvas enhances its impact.

By the time of the Holwell Carr bequest the Gallery had actively added to its original nucleus by purchases as well as gifts. Its administrative machinery was comparatively simple and — perhaps wisely — there was no planned policy of acquisitions. At first the Gallery had been administered by a Keeper with an assistant, but quite soon a "Committee of Six Gentlemen" was placed over him. This administrative structure has remained the same in essence, although the Gallery staff has now expanded into a series of departments responsible to a Director, and the Committee long ago became a Board of Trustees. It is difficult to trace exactly how, in the very early days, purchases were initiated; however, the results were often astonishing. In 1825 the gem-like, charming Correggio *The Madonna of the Basket* was bought. The following year the Gallery bought Titian's *Bacchus and Ariadne* (at present undergoing restoration) and the *Bacchanalian Dance* by Poussin — itself in part a homage to Titian. And in the course of the next few years such fine pictures as Correggio's *Mercury Instructing Cupid before Venus* and Murillo's *Two Trinities* were purchased.

Nevertheless, there was something random and haphazard about the conduct of the Gallery during that period. The Trustees sometimes met no more than once a year, and even when they did meet, no coherent or complete record of their deliberations was kept. There were problems connected with conserving the growing collection — both in cleaning the pictures and in finding space to exhibit them properly. The Trustees' policy — such as it was — of purchases was eventually attacked as too narrow and conservative. There was a good deal of truth in most of the accusations. It is most interesting to realize that the criticism reflected a new and serious concern with the purposes of a public collection of paintings. In 1837 Queen Victoria ascended the throne; in 1840 she married Prince Albert. With the coming of the Victorian Age, there was an increasing emphasis on education and a heightened historical awareness that benefited the Gallery. Prince Albert himself was deeply interested in painting, and did much to foster ideas about the value of museums.

It was in such a climate that a storm burst on the Gallery in 1853 — a storm that had long been heralded but which was directly caused by controversy over a group of cleaned pictures. The Gallery had then been in existence almost thirty years, and Mr. Angerstein's house had quickly proven too small to accommodate it. People began to find the building too hot and dirty both for their own enjoyment and for the good of the paintings. After some of the inevitable delays connected with all projects involving governments and government expenditure, the National Gallery was moved to a new building designed for it in Trafalgar Square by William Wilkins, a capable but not very inspired architect. In 1838 the newly-crowned Queen Victoria made an official visit to the collection in its new premises (which it shared with the Royal Academy until 1869). Not only did the new building house two institutions but living space was provided for the Keeper of the Gallery and his family — an arrangement that ended only after the Royal Academy moved out.

Perhaps it is not so surprising that Wilkins' new gallery was soon declared inadequate from the point of view of space and ventilation. London was a smoke-polluted city, and Trafalgar Square itself was not particularly salubrious. The pictures were crowded on the walls, and people crowded into the rooms — sometimes merely to lounge or seek shelter from bad weather. Dirty, dusty, foul are only a few of the adjectives used not about some Victorian slum but about the English national picture gallery in the 1840s. To these complaints must be added the increasingly serious criticism that no attention was being paid by the Trustees to earlier schools of painting, especially those of the fifteenth century, which had come to be recognized as no less great than the well-established High Renaissance. In an attempt to remedy the dirty appearance of the pictures, a group of them was cleaned in 1852. The resulting outcry was so strong that Parliament the next year appointed a Select Committee to inquire into all aspects of the Gallery: cleaning, accommodation, organization and purchasing policy. Facts both shocking and entertaining came to light, judicious reforms were proposed and implemented, and a new triumphant era began for the Gallery.

Yet, ironically, what had brought all this about was an outcry that the Trustees had allowed a group of important pictures (including *The Stonemason's Yard* and an ex-Angerstein Claude) to be ruined by cleaning. Not many years ago a rather similar cry was raised about other pictures. Such a reaction is perhaps inevitable whenever some familiar masterpiece changes in appearance after cleaning. But the inevitable change which follows removal of dirty varnish is not ruin. It is a hopeful sign that general public approval greeted the reappearance of Sebastiano del Piombo's *The Resurrection of Lazarus* after a major task of cleaning and restoration. The fact is that the pictures cleaned in 1852 were not ruined by the process; they hang in the Gallery today in remarkably good condition.

One positive result of the criticism, after the storm and the investigations, was a new constitution for the Gallery. In 1855 a director was appointed: Sir Charles Eastlake, who had previously served as Keeper and was then also President of the Royal Academy. Eastlake was a loyal public servant, a perceptive connoisseur and a scholar. The responsibility for purchasing pictures was given to him; he bought brilliantly, traveling in Europe in search of worthy acquisitions during his directorship, which ceased only at his death in 1865. The previous tendency had been to buy paintings by familiar well-established artists. It is very much due to the personal achievements of Eastlake that the early Italian pictures acquired were masterpieces as well as historically representative. Among his acquisitions were the Bronzino *Allegory*, the wonderful Veronese *Family of Darius*, Rogier van der Weyden's fragment from a larger picture of *The Magdalen Reading*, the beautiful Botticelli *Portrait of a Young Man*, Uccello's *Rout of San Romano* and — perhaps the most striking of all — *the Baptism of Christ* by Piero della Francesca, a painter who was scarcely known or appreciated. Today he is recognized as one of the great figures of the early Rennaissance. Few examples of his work are found outside of Italy, and the Gallery is uniquely fortunate in owning three of his superb works.

It was during Eastlake's directorship that the legal disputes resulting from Turner's will were finally settled. This meant that many of Turner's works, both oil paintings and water-colors, which he had bequeathed to the nation now entered the National Gallery. Today the Turner collection is divided among the National and Tate galleries and the British Museum. Some of Turner's finest paintings remain at Trafalgar Square, including the recently-cleaned *Sun Rising Through Vapor*, which Turner wished the Trustees to hang, with another of his pictures, between Claude's *Seaport* and *The Marriage of Isaac and Rebekah*. His wishes have been respected and the pictures hang in that arrangement.

Although the Tate Gallery is now established as the gallery of British art, it is worth noting that the National Gallery continues to exhibit a group of outstanding English paintings. These include Constable's very popular *Haywain*, some powerful portraits by Reynolds, and pictures by Gainsborough that extend over the range of his style and subject matter: from early landscapes like *Cornard Wood* to the later double portrait, *The Morning Walk*, with its delicate treatment of the strolling couple and the enchanted woodland setting. This master-piece was bought for the Gallery in 1954 with the financial help of the National Art-Collections Fund.

In many ways Eastlake's death in 1865 marked the end of an epoch. The Gallery had become established as a great national collection. Even schools of painting like the German, which were little esteemed outside their own country, had found a place in the Gallery. After the Prince Consort's death in 1861, Queen Victoria presented in his memory a group of German paintings, of which perhaps the rarest and most beautiful was Lochner's *SS. Matthew, Catherine and John the Evangelist*, part of an altarpiece once in a church at Cologne.

After 1865 there was no diminution of energy on the Gallery's behalf but, with increasing competition for masterpieces, prices were consequently rising. Eastlake's immediate successors — Sir William Boxall and Sir Frederic Burton — were still able to make some brilliant purchases. In 1871 the collection of Dutch and Flemish pictures formed by an earlier Prime Minister, Sir Robert Peel, was bought; it included two famous masterpieces, Rubens' *Le Chapeau de Paille* and Hobbema's *The Avenue, Middelharnis*. Both Rubens and Hobbema were, of course, familiar names to the nineteenth-century public. Almost totally forgotten until rediscovered by the critic Thoré was Jan Vermeer — the rarest of all Dutch painters and now one of the most prized. Thoré had owned Vermeer's *A Young Woman Standing at a Virginal*, which was bought for the Gallery in 1892, two years before Burton retired as director. Burton's twenty-year tenure saw many perceptive and superb purchases, distributed widely over the field of European art. Such pictures as Holbein's *The Ambassadors* and Velázquez' *Philip IV* — masterpieces by two very different portrait painters — were bought by Burton.

In 1894 responsibility for acquisitions was given to the Trustees, who were to be advised by the director. This major policy change did not lead to a decline in the quality of what was bought; inevitably, however, it has sometimes prevented the Gallery from benefiting from the sort of flair that Eastlake was free to exercise.

* * *

Throughout the first thirty or forty years of the present century the Gallery continued to acquire important pictures. In 1903 the National Art-Collections Fund was formed, a private body whose purpose is to save for the nation works of art of all kinds. The Fund was instrumental in keeping Holbein's *Duchess of Milan* in England; this picture was dramatically "saved" at the last moment by an anonymous donation of £40,000 toward its total cost of £72,000 — a high price for 1909, when the incident occurred. Although the model in this portrait was not English, she nearly married an English king, Henry VIII, for whom Holbein — as his court painter — must have painted the portrait. The Fund also played a part in the acquisition in 1929 of another treasure long associated with England, the *Wilton Diptych*, showing King Richard II in prayer before the Virgin and Child.

World War II brought about a total dislocation of the National Gallery's collection. Although the pictures were safely evacuated from London, the building was slightly damaged by bombing. Even without such damage, the building was clearly unsuited in many ways to properly house a great collection of paintings. A new director, Sir Philip Hendy, was appointed in 1946. He faced innumerable problems in the immediate post-war years — from a totally inadequate annual purchase grant to the urgent need for air-conditioned rooms. He initiated a thorough program of restoration and cleaning, and began the reconstruction of the building. Eventually, all rooms will be air-conditioned — a long-needed defense against the London climate and dust. At the same time, an equally overdue plan was initiated for the building of new exhibition rooms in the limited space available at the back of the Gallery. This "northern extension" to the Gallery has been fully planned, and the actual construction is underway.

The Gallery's personnel structure was also reorganized under Sir Hendy. A complete Conservation Department, as well as a Scientific Department and laboratory, was created so that pictures could be treated by the best modern methods. A modern gallery has also other duties to the general public and to scholars. A very active Publications Department today tries to cater to public demands by providing photographs, slides and colored postcards, as well as booklets to illustrate aspects of the collection or guide the visitor around it. Recently, "Soundguides" — tape-recorded tours — have been introduced. Since the nineteenth century, the Gallery has produced excellent historical and scholarly catalogs of its pictures. In that tradition, an unrivalled series of detailed catalogs has been published since 1945. The present director, Mr. Martin Davies, who succeeded Sir Philip Hendy in January, 1968, is himself the author of many of these catalogs.

Whatever other activities rightly find a place at the Gallery, its reputation ultimately depends on its acquisition of paintings. Some of the great masterpieces acquired many years ago for the National Gallery have already been mentioned. They represent a standard that provides a touchstone of quality. It must also be remembered that throughout the world serious study of art history has brought deeper understanding of certain artists and art movements that were often unfairly neglected. In England, a grave time-lag intervened before the greatness of the Impressionist and post-Impressionist painters was recognized. The Gallery suffered, and probably will always suffer, from that failure of understanding. It was fortunate, however, in receiving the bequest of Sir Hugh Lane in 1917 because that collection included one large-scale masterpiece by Renoir, *Les Parapluies*, and smaller, yet quite brilliant *plein-air* pictures by Manet and Degas: *La Musique aux Tuileries* and *Bains de Mer*.

During Sir Philip Hendy's directorship, many great paintings were acquired, notably in areas where the Gallery's representation had previously been weak. Some of these were straightforward purchases, such as Altdorfer's revolutionary *Landscape* — bringing to the Gallery a rare and poetic sixteenth-century painter. Other pictures of high quality were acquired under the provisions of a Government Finance Act, whereby very important works of art may be accepted by the state in lieu of death duties; in that way the Gallery obtained the movingly beautiful *Pietà* by Rogier van der Weyden. Yet it was the nineteenth-century French school, especially the work of those painters now recognized as forerunners of modern art, which most desperately needed strengthening. A number of paintings by Courbet, Monet and Renoir were added but in many ways the most striking was probably *Les Grandes Baigneuses* by Cézanne. Not only is this picture a significant monument that sums up Western tradition while looking prophetically to the future, but there is also hopeful significance in the method of its purchase. Its vast price was partly met out of the Gallery's limited funds, but supplemented by a special government grant and greatly aided by a magnificent gift from a private source, the Max Rayne Foundation. Thus the Gallery, whose beginnings owe so much to private benefactors' generosity, as well as to government good sense, was able through comparable means to add spectacularly to the national collection in 1964, one hundred and forty years after its creation.

Michael Levey

ITALY

DUCCIO. *Transfiguration.*

In 1308 Duccio was commissioned to paint a large altarpiece, now preserved in the cathedral museum of Siena. Three years later, the imposing work was carried in procession by the citizenry from Duccio's studio to the cathedral, where it was installed on the high altar. The little panel reproduced here was originally a part of this epic work; it shows the *Transfiguration* of Christ before the apostles Peter, John and James, and the prophets Moses and Elijah. Limpid and balanced, the composition is laid out on a rough, rocky peak. The gestures and glances of the apostles and prophets direct the viewer's attention to the figure of Christ at the central axis of the painting. The dense gold streaks of His red and blue robes reflect the glitter of the smooth gold ground. (G.D.R.)

DUCCIO DI BUONINSEGNA
Siena circa 1278–1318
Transfiguration (1311)
Tempera on panel; 17 1/4″ × 18″.
The lower part is in a poor state of preservation; the figure of John in the center is damaged. It is a predella panel originally on the reverse of the *Virgin in Majesty,* now in the cathedral museum, Siena. Acquired in Siena by R. H. Wilson and donated to the National Gallery in 1891.

PISANELLO. *The Vision of St. Eustace* and *The Virgin and Child with SS. George and Anthony Abbott.* pp. 20–21

Although presented in irrational and visionary terms, Pisanello's sophisticated narratives are not simply hedonistic but imply a profound disquietude, a morbidly pessimistic sense of life and destiny. It is this introspective drama that makes Pisanello a towering figure among the artists of the International Gothic style. His portraits possess an implacable realism, as evidenced by the two fabulous reveries reproduced here. Brave St. Eustace (page 20) is an elegant cavalier, wandering in a sacred wood that is also a royal park. St. George (page 21), in his lavish armor, is a sophisticated gentleman who remains imperturbable despite the bell ringing of the rural saint and the pale, tremulous aura of the Virgin. The naturalistic details, though acutely rendered, serve a mystical function: to lend truth to enchantments and mirages in order to obliterate awareness of the turbulence of Pisanello's time. (G.L.M.)

MASACCIO. *The Virgin and Child With Angels.* *p. 22*
The wooden throne, with its straight lines and sharply contoured moldings,
dominates the composition and defines and limits the space occupied by the
Virgin and Child. The rich blue mantle, falling in deep folds, exalts the two
20 principal figures, whose features are barely indicated. Squeezed in at the

sides of the throne, two angels establish the "reality" of the space around the central group. The two angel musicians in the foreground — whose sharply foreshortened instruments extend toward the outside of the picture — serve the same function. (G.D.R.)

MASACCIO
(TOMMASO GUIDI)
Castel S. Giovanni 1401 — Rome 1428
The Virgin and Child With Angels (1426)
Tempera on panel with rounded top;
53″ × 28 3/4″.
Some of the paint has been lost and parts
of the Madonna and the Child have been
restored. It was the central panel of an altar-
piece — documented and described by Va-
sari — which the artist executed for the
chapel of the notary Giuliano di Colino
degli Scarsi in the church of the Carmine at
Pisa. It was dismembered at the end of the
sixteenth century and its parts are now distributed among the National Gallery, the
Museo Nazionale of Pisa, the Capodimonte
Gallery in Naples, the state museums in
Berlin and the Lanckoronski collection in
Vienna. This panel was acquired from the
Woodburn and Sutton collections in 1916.

PAOLO UCCELLO. *St. George and the Dragon.*

In an earlier painting of this subject (now at the Musée Jacquemart André in Paris) a vast landscape extends behind the battling figures in the foreground. The compositional elements are identical in this later version, but here the cave and the trees blend into the clouds, delimiting the farther planes from the battle area. The figures of St. George and the dragon draw the eye along converging lines to the outer picture space. Slight suggestions of irony enliven the painting: the princess appears to be holding the dragon on a leash, and the saint's lance is unnaturally elongated. (G.D.R.)

PAOLO UCCELLO
(PAOLO DI DONO)
Florence 1397 — Florence 1475
St. George and the Dragon (circa 1455)
Tempera on canvas; 22 1/2″ × 28 3/4″.
Formerly in the Lanckoronski
collection in Vienna.

On pages 24–25:
PAOLO UCCELLO
Niccolò da Tolentino at the Battle of San Romano (circa 1456–60)
Tempera on panel; 5′11 3/4″ × 10′4 3/4″.
With two other panels showing related subjects, now in the Uffizi and the Louvre, it was originally in a room of the Medici Palace in Florence, where Vasari saw other unidentified works by Uccello and Pesellino. Formerly in the Giraldi and Lombardi-Baldi collections in Florence, it was acquired by the National Gallery in 1857.

23

PAOLO UCCELLO. *Niccolò da Tolentino at the Battle of San Romano.*

pp. 24–25

This panel probably represents the early stages of the 1432 battle between the Florentines and the Sienese near San Romano. The compositional movement starts at the left — with ranks of horsemen bearing lances, banners and trumpets — and thins out at the center, which is dominated by the Florentine condottiere, Niccolò da Tolentino, on a white horse. On the far right, a lone fighter, hampered by the weapons of two assailants, raises his battle club against a third enemy. A flowering hedge marks the limits of the foreground area, in which broken lances, shields and pieces of armor are laid out in a reticulated pattern that stresses the three-dimensional composition. Uccello's strong interest in geometric structure is matched by his obvious pleasure in depicting elaborate fabrics and heavy decorative and metallic elements. (G.D.R.)

PIERO DELLA FRANCESCA. *The Baptism of Christ.*

Piero has captured the moment in time just before the baptism of Christ. In absolute immobility, the figures and the smooth trees stand firmly planted; the dove is poised with spread wings; and the still water of the river reflects the lines and colors of the landscape. John the Baptist's rustic garb, the loincloth that barely covers Christ's robust body, the shirt the catechumen is pulling over his head as he undresses, and the angels' tunics — all fall in compact folds or are loosely gathered. The entire composition is homogeneous, and harmony reigns in this shining world. The light reveals the limpid volume of every element, traces the movements of the composition, and establishes the distances in the clearly defined space. (G.D.R.)

PIERO DELLA FRANCESCA
Borgo Sansepolcro circa 1410–
Borgo Sansepolcro 1492
The Baptism of Christ (circa 1440–50)
Tempera and oil on panel with rounded top; 65 3/4″ × 45 3/4″.
The surface is cracked and worn. Probably painted for the Priorato di S. Giovanni Battista in Sansepolcro, it was bought in 1857 by J. C. Robinson who in turn sold it to M. Uzielli. Acquired at the sale of the Uzielli collection in London, 1861.

PIERO DELLA FRANCESCA. *The Nativity.*

A strong network of metric and chromatic relationships connect the dis-associated elements of this scene. The figures, which are small in relation to the size of the panel, are in isolated positions and appear withdrawn into themselves. The child has been laid down far from his mother; she responds

PIERO DELLA FRANCESCA
The Nativity (circa 1470–75)
Tempera and oil on panel;
48 3/4″ × 48 1/2″.
The surface is badly rubbed because of a violent "cleaning" in the past. Some scholars believe that this is an unfinished work. It has been identified with one of the paintings

seen by Vasari at the house of the artist's heirs. From their descendants it passed to the Marini family. Eastlake saw it on exhibition at the Uffizi and bought it in 1861 for the Barker collection. Acquired by the National Gallery at the Barker sale in London in 1874.

Above: detail.

to the appeal of his outstretched arms with only a glance. The singing angels — reminiscent of Luca della Robbia's choir loft — stand in close ranks, unaware of the action. Joseph, seen in profile, sits silent and absorbed by his own thoughts; the shepherds, shown almost full face, are intent on the star (not represented in the picture). Toward the center, the ass and the ox are arranged in contrasting positions — the boldly foreshortened ox wedged into the narrow central space and the ass reaching into the space above. On either side of the foreshortened shed are glimpses of landscapes — trees, rocks and water on the left and a city (perhaps Sansepolcro) on the right — with no common plane linking them. (G.D.R.)

ALESSO BALDOVINETTI. *Portrait of a Lady in Yellow.*
Numerous artists, including Domenico Veneziano, Paolo Uccello and Pollaiolo, have been suggested as the painter of this fine portrait, but most contemporary authorities attribute it to Baldovinetti. The immobile figure is held within sharply defined contours incised on a deep blue ground. Her mouth is compressed, the glance fixed, and the skin taut on her face and neck. The necklace, the band of cloth with a pearl ornament in her hair, and the thin black cord that cuts across the convex brow emphasize the compactness of the volumes. Imperceptible vibrations, such as the slightly disarranged, glinting hair animate the figure. (G.D.R.)

COSIMO TURA. *The Virgin and Child Enthroned.* *p. 32*
This painting is exceptionally interesting as a document of the stylistic and cultural factors that influenced Tura. The psychological drama of Donatello's heroes and the metaphysical historicism of Mantegna interested him less than did their pictorial language, which he adapted by infusing them with esoteric significance and a kind of magic, or rather alchemy, a science in vogue at Ferrara. The elaborate rendering of architectural motifs and lush materials indicate that Tura's view of the world was matched by his extraordinary skill as a technician. (G.L.M.)

ANDREA MANTEGNA. *The Agony in the Garden.* *p. 33*
A useful comparision can be made between this work and a painting of the same subject by Mantegna's brother-in-law, Giovanni Bellini. The two paintings hang side by side in the National Gallery. Bellini's version is based on a warm, embracing feeling for nature and is set in a broad landscape. Its drama is limited to specific events. Mantegna's composition, on the other

ALESSO BALDOVINETTI
Florence 1427 — Florence 1499
Portrait of a Lady in Yellow (circa 1465)
Tempera on panel; 24 3/4″ × 15 3/4″.
Traditionally identified as the Countess
Palma of Urbino and subsequently as Fran-
cesca Stati, the wife of the poet Angelo
Galli of Urbino. A more recent suggestion,
based on the device embroidered on the
sleeve, identifies the subject as a sister of
Piero Soderini. It was acquired in 1866 from
the Florentine dealer Egidi.

COSIMO TURA
Ferrara 1430 — Ferrara circa 1497
The Virgin and Child Enthroned
(circa 1474)
Tempera on panel; 3′4 1/4″ × 7′10″.
This is the central panel of the Roverella altarpiece from the church of S. Giorgio Fuori, Ferrara. Other extant parts are the lunette from above the central panel (Louvre); part of the right-hand wing (Colonna collection); part of the left-hand wing (formerly in a private collection in London); and three tondos from the predella (Metropolitan Museum, Gardner Collection and Fogg Museum). Bought for the National Gallery in 1867.

hand, is charged with intellectual meanings expressed in a narrative style. The lapidary images, the statuesque immobility and the unequivocal narration are as controlled as in a stage production. Because it is so intensely allusive, Mantegna's art has been called "metaphysical." (G.L.M.)

ANTONELLO DA MESSINA.   *Christ Crucified.*   p. 34
This work is similar in theme to Antonello's *Crucifixion* of 1475, now in Antwerp. The mourners are shown here at a later moment of the drama: since Christ is dead, they no longer cry their grief but are caught in a deep inner melancholy. Behind them, atmospheric perspective reveals an immense landscape, stretching to infinity. Underlying the harmony of the composition and the gradation of colors is a system of proportions regulating the relationships among the mourners in the foreground, the landscape in the background and the figure of Christ against the open sky. The invisible architecture gives the work an inevitable, timeless quality. (G.L.M.)

ANTONELLO DA MESSINA.   *St. Jerome in His Study.*   p. 35
The rigidly centralized perspective in this painting recalls similar North Italian works by Jacopo Bellini and Mantegna, in which Tuscan perspective became an important element in the narrative. In his attempt to express

ANDREA MANTEGNA
Isola di Carturo 1431 — Mantua 1506
The Agony in the Garden (circa 1455)
Tempera on panel; 31 1/2″ × 24 3/4″.
Signed: OPVS/ANDREAE/MANTEGNA.
The oldest documented provenance is the
Aldobrandini collection in Rome, in the
seventeenth century. Bought by the National
Gallery in 1894.

a unitary conception of space, Antonello has stressed the impact of the
mystical elements. But the special magic of this painting lies in the complex
play of counterpoised lights that generate a series of contrasts which animate
the apparently motionless scene. The effects of light and shadow culminate
in the boxed-in room that dramatizes the mullioned window opening to an
azure sky. (G.L.M.)

ANTONELLO DA MESSINA
Messina 1430 — Messina 1479
Christ Crucified
Oil on panel; 10″ × 17 3/4″.
Signed and dated: *1475/ antonellus Messaneus/me pinxit* (Antonello of Messina painted me).
The panel was formerly rounded at the top. Bought through the Clarke Fund in 1884.

ANTONELLO DA MESSINA
St. Jerome in His Study (circa 1474)
Oil on lime panel; 14 1/4″ × 18″.
Cited by Michiel as in Venice around 1592. Bought by the museum in 1894.

GIOVANNI BELLINI. *The Agony in the Garden.*

Mantegna's system of form and spiritual values had a profound influence on Bellini. In Mantegna's robust compositions, Bellini found inspiration for the melancholy poetic qualities he employed to depict the beauty of nature. This painting so closely resembles Mantegna's panel of the same subject — especially in the figure of Christ — that it may be considered a brilliant contemporary variation on that work. Bellini's new vision of vast space, in which the dawn light conveys deeply felt emotion, is beautifully expressed in this panel. The apostles, sunk in an almost animal sleep, boldly embody a tormented psychological drama. (A.P.)

36

GIOVANNI BELLINI
Venice circa 1426 — Venice circa 1516
The Agony in the Garden (1458–59)
Panel; 32″ × 50″.
In the eighteenth century it was first identified as being in Consul Smith's collection in Venice. It then figured in Sir Joshua Reynolds' collection as a work of Mantegna. Waagen ascribed it to Bellini in 1859, when he saw it in the collection of the Reverend W. Davenport Bromley, from which the National Gallery acquired it in 1863.

GIOVANNI BELLINI. *The Blood of the Redeemer.*
This sensitive work belongs to Bellini's early period, and shows a subtle and religious feeling grafted onto the structural elements he adopted from Mantegna. The master's influence is seen in the boldness of the forms and the elaboration of the space, as well as in the cultivated allusions of the classical reliefs on the parapet. But the linear sensitivity and complex spiritual content are Bellini's innovations. An allegorical device is visible in the treatment of the landscape, which is divided into two contrasting parts. On one side there is an arid hill with ruined buildings; on the other, a thriving town whose towers rise toward a crystalline sky. (A.P.)

GIOVANNI BELLINI
The Blood of the Redeemer
Panel; 18 1/2″ × 13 1/2″.
Acquired in England in 1887. In 1464 the Pope forbade any discussion of the cult of the blood of Christ, but Carpaccio painted a similar subject in the early sixteenth century. It is likely that Bellini's painting was executed between 1460 and 1462.

GIOVANNI BELLINI. *The Madonna of the Meadow*.

This painting was assigned to various artists until 1929, when Gronau finally identified it as a work of Bellini's. The sweetly defined group is composed in a pyramidal form that seems to anticipate Raphael. But in contrast to the enveloping space modulated by sinuous contours in Raphael's landscapes, here a morning light illuminates a stretch of definite, almost identifiable countryside — in which men go about their daily tasks while the Madonna watches over her Child's sleep. (A.P.)

GIOVANNI BELLINI. *The Doge Leonardo Loredan*.

The spirituality and timelessness of this portrait is unusual. Very different from the artist's outdoor scenes, with their vibrant atmosphere and changing skies, this painting has a crystalline clarity. The portrait conveys the indomitable energy of the Doge, who was elected at the age of 65, and guided the Venetian Republic "with more than human valor" during the turbulent years from 1501 to 1521. (A.P.)

CARLO CRIVELLI. *The Annunciation With St. Emidius.*
In this extraordinary variation of the theme of the Annunciation, St. Emidius, the patron saint of a local cult, is seen beside the angel. Crivelli used his vivid imagination in the creation of a rich and detailed architectural setting in the Paduan style. The orchestration of color and the sensual quality of the lush materials are complemented by such realistic details as the household wares, the fluttering doves, the carnation plant, and the curious child peering around the parapet. (A.P.)

40

CARLO CRIVELLI
Venice circa 1430 — Ascoli circa 1493
The Annunciation With St. Emidius
Panel, transferred to canvas;
6′9 1/2″ × 4′9 1/2″.
Signed: OPUS. CAROLI. CRIVELLI/
VENETI and dated 1486.
From the church of the SS. Annunziata in Ascoli Piceno, this panel was commissioned to celebrate the concession of a privilege by Pope Sixtus IV on March 25, 1482. Removed in the Napoleonic period and taken to the Brera, it was in England by the mid-nineteenth century. Lord Taunton donated it to the Gallery in 1864.

BRAMANTINO. *The Adoration of the Kings.*

BRAMANTINO
(BARTOLOMEO SUARDI)
Lombardy circa 1460–1536
The Adoration of the Kings
Oil on poplar panel; 22 1/2" × 21 3/4".
It is not known where the artist was born
and died. He was a pupil of Bramante in
Milan. Bramantino was also an architect, the
greatest among his Lombard contemporaries.
Bought by Sir A. H. Layard from the Man-
frin collection in Venice around 1860, the
panel came to the Gallery with the Layard
bequest in 1916.

One of Bramantino's major works, this painting was completed before his first visit to Rome in 1508. Early in his career, Bramantino's color range derived mainly from the Lombard masters of the previous generation — especially Butinone and Foppa. But the liberating influence of Bramante, the great master from whom he takes his nickname, became evident in his mature style. Bramante's measured, monumental rhythm also affected the disposition and movement of the figures in this painting, as well as their relationship to the architectural framework. The intense coloristic effects of Bramantino's youth are replaced here by clear, calm tones. (R.M.)

41

ANTONIO POLLAIOLO
(ANTONIO BENCI)
Florence circa 1431 — Rome 1498
Apollo and Daphne (circa 1470–75)
Tempera on panel; 11 1/2″ × 7 3/4″.
Bought in Rome by W. Cunningham in 1845;
at the sale of his collection in 1849, it was
acquired by White. It came to the National
Gallery in 1876, as a bequest of W. Ellis.

ANTONIO POLLAIOLO. *Apollo and Daphne.*

The myth of Apollo's pursuit of Daphne — in which the nymph is transformed into a laurel tree just as the god is about to seize her — stimulated Pollaiolo's imagination. Although fascinated by the relationship between man and nature, he did not stress the more savage and primordial aspects of the myth. The youth and tenderness of the two figures and the refinement of their costumes reveal the artist's intention to relate the episode

ANTONIO POLLAIOLO
The Martyrdom of St. Sebastian
Tempera on panel; 9′6 1/2″ × 6′7 1/2″.
The panel has probably been cut down at the
sides. The artist was assisted on this painting
by his brother Paolo. According to an old
tradition, Gino di Lodovico Capponi was the
model for the figure of St. Sebastian. Vasari
states that the painting was commissioned in
1475 by Antonio Pucci for his family chapel
(Oratorio di S. Sebastiano) in the church of
the SS. Annunziata in Florence. Acquired
from the Marchese Roberto Pucci in 1857.

in "courtly" terms. The vibrant intensity of the picture is created by the diagonal impetus animating the figures, who almost seem to be suspended in air. There is also a dramatic charge in the leafy branches held in the nymph's outstretched arms as she recoils from the god's embrace. (G.D.R.)

ANTONIO POLLAIOLO. *The Martyrdom of St. Sebastian.* *p. 43*
Assisted by his brother Piero, the artist created a composition in two parts — foreground and background — which he chose not to fuse into a single whole. In the narrow rocky foreground, the beginning of the saint's martyrdom is shown: the archers, bending their bows or stooping to set their arrows, enclose the saint, bound to the upper part of a tree trunk, in a solidly constructed pyramid of forms. Beyond the edge of the slope, a broad tree-dotted valley, along which winds a river, stretches to the ring of misty mountains. The distant peaks blurring into the sky suggest limitless space. The natural elements of sparkling water and opaque yellow-brown countryside dominate the landscape. The horsemen, their rearing horses, and the ruined triumphal arch are an integral part of this grandiose interpretation of the Arno Valley. (G.D.R.)

SANDRO BOTTICELLI. *Mystic Nativity.*
The allegorical figures, symbols and inscriptions in this painting have created considerable controversy among scholars. Botticelli expressed the doubts and problems that beset his maturity in such elements as the prophetic Greek inscription along the upper edge of the picture: "this picture at the end of the year 1500, during the troubles in Italy, I, Alessandro, painted in the interval after the time, during the fulfillment of the Eleventh Chapter of St. John, in the second woe of the Apocalypse, in the loosing of the devil for three and a half years, who will then be chained up in the Twelfth Chapter and we shall see him (. . . .) as in the present painting." Botticelli's allusion to "troubles in Italy" probably refers to the disturbances in Florence after the death of Lorenzo the Magnificent: invasion by the French, the collapse of the republic established by Savonarola, Cesare Borgia's menacing program of expansion. The scene recalls Savonarola's sermons, for at Christmas he had appealed to the Florentines to rally in unison around the Manger. Satan, repelled and downtrodden, is seen with other demons in the grassy foreground. The three angels dressed in white, pink and green, who watch over the hut, represent the theological virtues of Hope, Faith and Charity. They are also derived from Savonarola, as are the angels gathered in a circle, singing hymns and bearing olive wreaths and branches. (G.D.R.)

SANDRO BOTTICELLI
(ALESSANDRO FILIPEPI)
Florence 1445 — Florence 1510
Mystic Nativity (circa 1501)
Acquired by W. Y. Ottley at the sale of the Villa Aldobrandini in Rome at the beginning of the 19th century. After changing hands several times it entered the Fuller Maitland collection, and in 1878 it was bought by Smith for the National Gallery.

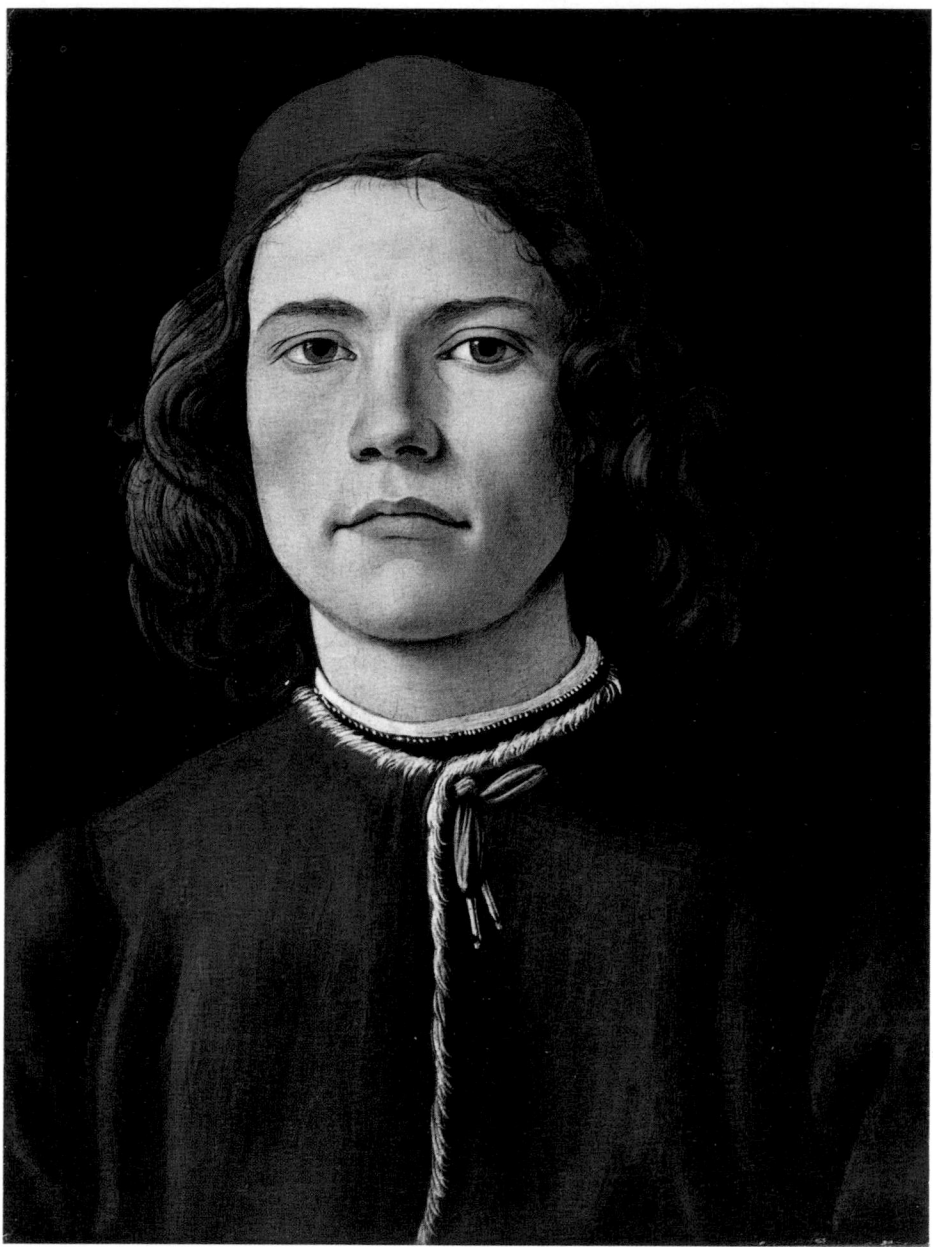

SANDRO BOTTICELLI. *Portrait of a Young Man.*
Among the numerous portraits by Botticelli, this one is remarkable for its aggressive quality. Despite his rather static frontal stance, the youth seems to have appeared unexpectedly or to have turned abruptly toward the observer. He looks out rather haughtily, with his chin raised slightly and his jaws set, as his wavy locks below the red cap sway softly. (G.D.R.)

SANDRO BOTTICELLI. *Venus and Mars.*
In Botticelli's version of the well-known ancient myth, Venus' beauty and fascination have conquered the proud god of war. While he lies deep in sleep, infant satyrs ridicule him and steal his helmet and lance. The references to contemporary and ancient literary sources are subtle and not

SANDRO BOTTICELLI
Venus and Mars (circa 1475–80)
Tempera on panel; 27 1/4″ × 68″.
The panel was probably executed for the
Vespucci family, since wasps appear on the
far right of the picture and "wasp" is *vespa*
in Italian. Bought in Florence by A. Barker,
it was acquired by the National Gallery at
the sale of his collection in London in 1874.

readily disentangled. They include Lorenzo the Magnificent, Politian, Reposiano and Lucretius, and Neo-Platonic themes, in particular Ficino's *Venus Humanitas,* in which hate and discord are appeased. Botticelli's interpretation of the theme is very free and shows a classicizing nostalgia in the studied position of the goddess. In his portrayal of Mars, however, the artist has departed from tradition: the warrior god has been transformed into a lean-limbed adolescent with feminine features. (G.D.R.)

PIERO DI COSIMO. *A Mythological Subject.* p. 47

According to Ovid's *Metamorphoses,* Cephalus, son of Hermes, unintentionally killed his wife Procris while out hunting. Procris, an Athenian princess, had given him an infallible lance and a trained dog that had belonged to Artemis. Although most scholars identify this panel with the Procris myth, the unjustified presence of the satyr presents certain problems. In the green, brown and blue landscape everything is motionless. The satyr and the dog are silent and melancholy participants in the scene, as if fearing to disturb the peace of the soft body lying among the flowers. Although the wound was fatal, it is shown as a pinprick. Only two trickles of blood mark the breast and the bent arm of the dying young woman. (G.D.R.)

LEONARDO DA VINCI. *The Virgin and Child, St. Anne and the Infant St. John.*

This drawing poses a complicated question of identification. In a letter to Isabella d'Este on April 8, 1501, Fra Pietro da Novellara described a study executed by Leonardo for an altarpiece commissioned by the Servites of Florence. It is likely that Leonardo's *Virgin and Child with St. Anne,* now in the Louvre, is the altarpice in question, but the work minutely described in the monk's letter differs in many respects from both this cartoon in the National Gallery and the picture in Paris. Since it is known that the London cartoon came from Milan, it may have been the study for an earlier version of the painting, now lost. In any event, the cartoon has always, as Vasari tells us, been considered a great work of art. On its completion, it was put on exhibition and attracted admiring crowds. Certainly it is one of the most important works in the development of sixteenth-century art. The unusual composition — in which the figures make a composite form but keep their identity, and the limited space is made to seem broad — influenced painters from Raphael, Fra Bartolomeo and Andrea del Sarto to the Mannerists. Leonardo's new departure, along with Raphael's paintings of the Holy Family and Michelangelo's *Holy Family,* established the classicism of the High Renaissance. (R.M.)

LEONARDO DA VINCI
Vinci 1452 — Amboise 1519
The Virgin and Child, St. Anne and the Infant St. John (circa 1500)
Charcoal on paper; 54 3/4" × 39 3/4".
From the Resta collection in Milan, it passed to the Marchese Casnedi's collection in the late seventeenth century. In 1722 it was bought by the Sagredo family of Venice, from whom Robert Udny, brother of the English ambassador to Venice, bought it in 1763. In 1791 it appeared in an inventory of the Royal Academy. Bought by the National Gallery from the Royal Academy in 1966.

MICHELANGELO. *The Entombment.*

The attribution of this unfinished painting — with blanks on the right for the Virgin and above for the tomb — to Michelangelo is questioned by some critics. Yet even those scholars who assign it to Battista Franco or a hypothetical Master of Manchester (after the Madonna of the same name), do not deny that Michelangelo had an important role in its execution. According to an undocumented tradition, the idea for the composition of *The Entombment* derives from Mantegna. But there is a more obvious iconographic connection with Dürer, in the splendid tension of the central group of St. John, a Holy Woman, and Joseph of Arimathaea supporting the figure of Christ. (R.M.)

PIETRO PERUGINO. *St. Michael* and *St. Raphael and Tobias.* p. 52

These two panels have undergone considerable alterations. A strip added to the top and another removed from the bottom damaged *St. Michael* in particular. The figure of Satan, originally at his feet, was painted over. Despite such changes, the artist's compositional virtuosity is still recognizable. Perugino adopted a composed and carefully calibrated solution for *St. Michael,* and a freer and more asymmetrical scheme for *St. Raphael and Tobias.* (G.D.R.)

RAPHAEL. *Vision of a Knight.*   p. 53

The most likely explanation of this picture is that it represents Scipio's *Dream,* a moralizing allegory that recurs in Florentine Neo-Platonism. Thus it may be read as showing Scipio torn between Pallas Athena's offer of distinction in knowledge and arms, and the more earthy rewards of Aphrodite. The painting probably belonged to a diptych, the other half of which is the little panel of *The Three Graces,* at Chantilly, which shows them presenting the apples of Hesperides to the victor. This painting, once held

MICHELANGELO
(MICHELANGELO BUONARROTI)
Caprese 1475 — Rome 1564
The Entombment (1506–11)
Oil on panel; 62 1/2" × 58 3/4".
Michelangelo was active in Florence and Rome as both a sculptor and architect. Formerly in the Farnese collection, the panel was bought by the National Gallery in 1868.

PIETRO PERUGINO
(PIETRO VANNUCCI)
Città della Pieve 1445 — Fontignano 1523
St. Michael and *St. Raphael and Tobias*
(circa 1499)
Oil on panel with rounded top;
each panel 49 1/2″ × 22 3/4″.
The two panels have been altered by additions, repainting and restorations. Two old copies of the works in the Eghenter collection, Milan, show how the originals looked. Some scholars believe that the painting is in part the work of the young Raphael.
Perugino's signature appears in the lower left-hand corner of the *St. Michael:* PETRUS PERUSINU(S) PINXIT. With four other panels it formed an altarpiece commissioned by the Certosa of Pavia in 1496 and probably delivered at the end of 1499, on the urging of Ludovico il Moro. When the Carthusian order was suppressed in 1782, the altarpiece was dismembered and some of the panels were exhibited at the Accademia di Brera. Acquired by the National Gallery from Duke Ludovico Melzi in 1856.

to be one of Raphael's earliest works, is now dated around 1505, after the artist moved to Florence. It is unlikely that the composition could have preceded Raphael's *Marriage of the Virgin,* painted in 1504. In that work, as in this, the forms are smoothly continuous with the space, so that all structural elements are in harmony. (R.M.)

RAPHAEL. *Madonna and Child with SS. John the Baptist and Nicholas of Bari ("The Ansidei Madonna").* p. 54

The illegible date on the drapery below the Madonna's left hand has led to considerable controversy over this painting. According to current opinion, it was begun around 1504, before Raphael moved to Florence, and completed in 1506, during his brief return to Perugia. Florentine influence,

52

RAPHAEL
(RAFFAELLO SANZIO)
Urbino 1483 — Rome 1520
Vision of a Knight (circa 1505)
Oil on panel; 6 3/4″ × 6 3/4″.
This panel, with *The Three Graces* at the Condé Museum at Chantilly, belonged to the Borghese collection in Rome. At the end of the eighteenth century it was in the Ottley collection, then changed hands several times. Bought by the Gallery in 1847.

RAPHAEL
St. Catherine of Alexandria
Oil on panel; 28″ × 20 3/4″.
This may be the painting that Pietro Aretino,
in a letter of August, 1550, said he sent to
Agosto d'Adda. A preliminary drawing is in
the Louvre. Day acquired it from the Bor-
ghese collection around 1795, after which
it was taken to England. Bought by the
National Gallery in 1839.

RAPHAEL
*Madonna and Child with SS. John the
Baptist and Nicholas of Bari*
("*The Ansidei Madonna*")
Oil on panel; 9′ × 4′11 3/4″.
This panel was painted in 1506 for the An-
sidei Chapel of the church of San Fiorenzo
dei Serviti. Acquired in 1764 by Lord Robert
Spencer, who replaced it with a copy by Bin-
cola Monti. In the Duke of Marlborough's
collection until 1885, when it was bought by
the National Gallery.

especially the work of Fra Bartolomeo, is strong in both subject and composition. The figures are placed in a continuous rhythm, the architecture
is detailed with great precision, and the color — refracted and direct —
has great purity. Above all, time of day and light are stated with feeling,
and are abstractly modulated. (R.M.)

RAPHAEL. *St. Catherine of Alexandria.*
This magnificent painting is one of the major examples of the new "serpentine" form in the High Renaissance. It was executed at Florence in 1506–
07, the years when the artist was most interested in Leonardo's repertory
of forms and manner of painting. It is from Leonardo — perhaps his *Leda*
— that the strong torsion of the figure of the saint and the subtle filtered
effect of the light are derived. What Raphael has originated is the measured
correspondence of figure and landscape, in which the figure is the supporting element of an architectural structure.

ANDREA DEL SARTO. *Portrait of a Young Man.*

This famous painting may be a portrait of the sculptor Baccio Bandinelli, a friend of Andrea's. The object he is holding appears to be a block of stone; however, it is more likely that it is a book. There is a marked similarity between the features of this figure and those of the so-called self-portrait and the St. John in the *Madonna of the Harpies* (both in the Uffizi). Evidently the master used his own face as a masculine model, just as he adopted the features of his wife, Lucrezia del Fede, for all his women. The picture was probably executed in 1517–18, crucial years in the artist's development that culminated in the creation of the *Madonna of the Harpies* and the *Disputation on the Holy Trinity* (Pitti Palace, Florence). This por-

57

trait is the poetic highpoint of the period. In pose and characterization, worked out in a series of splendid preliminary drawings now in the Uffizi, there is a sensual and emotional quality that is carried on a clear architectonic structure. Head and torso turn in a succession of precisely defined planes, and the hands frame the block-like form of the stone or book. Shadowy effects derived from Leonardo — such as the eye sockets, from which a questioning, almost forlorn glance emerges — have been transmuted into a sensual, bitter awareness.

PONTORMO. *Joseph in Egypt.* p. 57

A typical example of Florentine tradition up to the early sixteenth century, this panel shows a series of scenes from the life of Joseph in one composition. Thus we see, simultaneously, Joseph's family at the court of Pharaoh, the people asking for bread, and the death of Jacob. The different episodes are presented on separate spatial planes but are interconnected by the swift rhythm of the composition in its counterpoint between the winding movement of the architecture and the restless, at times dreamlike, movements of the figures. This painting was part of a chamber decorated for Pierfrancesco Borgherini by Pontormo, Andrea del Sarto, Bachiacca and Granacci. The young Pontormo was still strongly influenced by his master, Andrea del Sarto, with whom he shared an interest in Northern prints and drawings — in particular those of Lucas van Leyden. However, a comparison with the two excellent paintings by Andrea for the Camera Borghini (Pitti Palace), reveals the younger artist's anti-classical bent, which seems to prophesy the new current of Mannerism.

BRONZINO. *Allegory of Time and Love.*

Bronzino has depicted a typical Counter-Reformation allegory. Time, the old man with the hourglass, and Truth, the woman in the opposite upper corner, draw the veil — a blue curtain — to reveal a complex group representing the vanity of luxury or the pleasures of love. Behind the central figures of Venus, Cupid and Pleasure are representatives of the vices they

BRONZINO
(AGNOLO DI COSIMO)
Florence 1503 — Florence 1572
Allegory of Time and Love
Oil on panel; 61" × 56 3/4".
Bronzino was the chief Mannerist portrait painter of the Medicean court. The panel was given to the King of France by Cosimo I, the first Grand Duke of Tuscany, who probably commissioned it.

CORREGGIO
(ANTONIO ALLEGRI)
Correggio 1489 — Correggio 1534
Mercury Instructing Cupid before Venus
(circa 1525)
Oil on canvas; 35 3/4" × 61".
The painting has been cut down on the right.
Corrections were made by the artist on the
right hip and the left foot of Venus. In other
copies of the painting, there is a quiver with
arrows by Venus' right foot, and Mercury's
drapery is different.
Bought for the Gallery in 1834.

GIORGIONE
Castelfranco circa 1477 — Venice 1510
Landscape with Figures (circa 1505)
Canvas; 28 3/4″ × 35 3/4″.
Discovered in poor condition in 1933 in the
Villa Garzone at Ponte Casale, it was im-
mediately bought by an English collector.
Acquired by the Gallery in 1960, it was care-
fully cleaned of old varnish and restored.

generate: on the left behind Cupid, Jealousy tears her hair; behind Pleasure, sweet-faced Deceit has the body of a griffon, with clawed feet and a
scaly tail. Deceit's hands are reversed, so that she seems to offer with her
right hand what she is offering with her left, and vice versa. In one hand
she holds a honeycomb, in the other her tail, which has a sting in it. At her
feet are the masks of a young woman and an old man. The cool, enamel-
like brilliance of the flesh depersonalizes the figures, annulling the sensuality
of the scene and eliminating any possible ambiguity. (R.M.)

CORREGGIO.   *Mercury Instructing Cupid before Venus.*
This painting may have formed a pair with the *Antiope* in the Duke of
Mantua's collection (now in the Louvre). They would have represented,
respectively, "intellectual love" and "physical love." Both belong to the   61

phase of the artist's career during which he was gradually approaching the triumphant sensuality characteristic of his mature work. The structure and the narrative are immersed in a voluptuous mist that may derive from Leonardo. Instead of tending toward shadow and dark feelings, however, it strives toward joy and light. (G.L.M.)

GIORGIONE. *Landscape with Figures.* p. 61

The meaning of this painting is ambiguous. The central group may represent the parable of the Good Samaritan, the miracle of St. Anthony, or

TITIAN
Pieve di Cadore circa 1488 — Venice 1576
Portrait of a Man (circa 1511–12)
Canvas; 32″ × 26″.
The painting bears the initials T. V. (Tiziano Vecelli), and may have belonged to van Dyck. It was famous in the seventeenth century and was known to Rembrandt and Sandrart. It was acquired from the descendants of Lord Darnley in 1904.

TITIAN
"Noli Me Tangere" (circa 1511–12)
Canvas; 43″ × 35 3/4″.
Cited as in the Muselli collection in Verona,
by Ridolfi. At the end of the eighteenth cen-
tury, it was in various French collections.
Bought by Samuel Rogers, who donated it
to the Gallery in 1856.

St. Roch being treated by the Good Gerald. Its connection to the battle
between St. George and the dragon is also unclear. In addition to its unusual subject matter, the painting is significant for its depiction of a magnificent twilight landscape in which monsters, saints and heroes take on
reality. Still Bellini-like in their refinement, the figures are immersed in a
subtle atmosphere and stand out against fantastic geological formations. On
the left rises a superb clump of trees with a tactile density that recalls
Titian. This work probably dates from shortly after the *Castelfranco Madonna* and before the monumental *Three Philosophers*. (A.P.)

TITIAN. *Portrait of a Man.* p. 62

Although Titian's initials appear on the parapet, many scholars in the past have attributed the painting to Giorgione. In fact, Giorgione's influence is very strong, and there is general agreement that Titian must have painted it in his youth, soon after his frescoes in Padua. A new violence is seen in the separation of the perspective planes, which is quite different from Giorgione's refined modulation of tones. New also is the compressed energy of the closed form — modeled by the light — which is created by the position of the arm. The cold tonality of the flow of gray-blue silk is the key to the color orchestration. The figure — which may be a self-portrait — is calm and serene, although his absent glance suggests a somewhat cold and disdainful attitude. (R.P.)

TITIAN. *"Noli Me Tangere."* p. 63

In spirit this painting is very close to the *Concert Champetre* in the Louvre — especially in the sumptuously rich tonality of the landscape and in the interdependence of the figures, the psychological mood and the surrounding landscape. Critics have alternately attributed both works to Giorgione and Titian; some scholars maintain that they are late works by Giorgione, which Titian finished. Such an explanation may be true of the *Concert* but here Titian's hand is evident even in the underlying sketch, which X-ray examination reveals has the same hesitations and corrections as the painting itself. The rich tonality and the dense pigment are typical of Titian's early period. The landscape with the group of buildings on the hill is identical with the landscape in Giorgione's Dresden *Venus*. According to a contemporary diarist, Marcantonio Michiel, this passage was painted by Titian, who was then assisting Giorgione. (R.P.)

TITIAN. *Venus and Adonis.*

Some scholars hold that this composition was the model for the canvas (now in the Prado) sent by Prince Philip of Spain to London in 1554, which remained in Titian's studio until it was acquired by Tintoretto. A close study of the organization of color and form shows, however, that this painting is instead a replica of the Prado painting. This is possible, since Titian expressed his great pleasure with the work in the letter that accompanied it to Spain. He therefore may have wished to keep a copy of it at home. Ludovico Dolce, who wrote admiringly of Titian, praised the picture for its naturalism; what is more apparent today is its lyrical transformation of reality. The atmosphere in this pagan fable of Adonis' departure toward death is charged with dramatic presentiment; at the same time, its warmth gives body to the two figures, whose Manneristic composition recalls Giulio Romano. The low-keyed, opulent light produces grainy tonalities. The quivering dogs add a domestic note that heightens the sensual warmth of the whole. (R.P.)

TITIAN
Venus and Adonis (circa 1554)
Canvas; 69 3/4″ × 73 1/2″.
Acquired from the Palazzo Colonna in Rome, the painting was taken to England in the early nineteenth century. It came to the Gallery with the Angerstein collection in 1824. Several versions are known, of which two are considered to be by Titian's own hand.

TITIAN. *The Vendramin Family.*

This splendid votive canvas represents Andrea Vendramin, his seven sons and his brother Gabriele adoring the reliquary of the True Cross, which is set on an altar between two lighted candles. The reliquary had been given in 1369 by Philippe de Meizière, Chancellor of the Kingdom of Cyprus, to an earlier Andrea Vendramin, who was chancellor of the Scuola di S. Giovanni Evangelista. It is probable that Gabriele, an enthusiastic collector, commissioned the painting in 1547 on the death of his brother Andrea, namesake of the ancestor who brought the reliquary into the family. (Gentile Bellini's painting in the Accademia of Venice shows the earlier Andrea miraculously recovering the reliquary after it had fallen into a canal.) A novel aspect of Titian's work is that the commemorative scene takes place in the open, and not in the Scuola di S. Giovanni Evangelista, where the reliquary was kept. The atmosphere is vibrant with human and religious feeling, while the cheerful afternoon light sets the scene in time.

TITIAN
The Vendramin Family (circa 1547)
Canvas; 6'9" × 9'10 1/2".
The painting was bought around 1630 by van Dyck. Shortly after van Dyck's death, it was acquired by the Earl of Northumberland and in 1929 it was sold by his descendants to the Gallery.
Above, oppposite: detail.

Composed in groups of threes, the figures are arranged so that the elders stand out against the sky and the youngsters appear at the sides. The three boys at the left have been captured in natural poses, while the major interest is focused on the youngest boy on the right, who is wearing red stockings and holding a little dog. (R.P.)

JACOPO TINTORETTO. *Portrait of Vincenzo Morosini.*

Vincenzo Morosini, a senator, served as prefect of Bergamo and president of the University of Padua. The gold stole on his shoulder was a high award for civic merit, and could have been earned only at a mature age. Tintoretto does not flatter his subject, but has emphasized his moral strength and suggested a defensive attitude as well as a somewhat disdainful solitude. This psychological intuition is complemented by the careful composition of the forms.

JACOPO TINTORETTO
Venice 1518 — Venice 1594
Portrait of Vincenzo Morosini (circa 1580)
Canvas; 33″ × 20″.
It was bought in 1922 by the dealer Agnew of London from the Contini collection in Rome. Donated to the National Gallery on the occasion of its centenary in 1924.

JACOPO TINTORETTO. *The Origin of the Milky Way.*

The composition of this magnificent painting has been unbalanced by the removal of a strip at the bottom, and layers of darkened varnish have dimmed the colors. But the fantasy of the sixteenth-century bed and curtain floating among the clouds and stars remains a superb example of Tintoretto's genius. Zeus, who appears here in the form of an eagle, instructs Hermes to smuggle the infant Hercules to his sleeping wife's breast, so that the child may become immortal by drinking her milk. Hera awakes, springs out of bed, and her milk is scattered into the sky, thus creating the

68

JACOPO TINTORETTO
The Origin of the Milky Way (1577–78)
Canvas; 50 1/4″ × 65″.
Probably painted for the Emperor Rudolph II, this canvas was acquired in 1890 from the Earl of Darnley, to whose predecessors it had belonged since 1828.

Milky Way. This is perhaps the most sensuous of Tintoretto's works, for he generally painted purely religious themes for churches, guild halls and government buildings. The flying figure of Hermes is one of the artist's most inventive compositional devices. (A.P.)

JACOPO TINTORETTO. *St. George and the Dragon.*

What is immediately striking about this painting is the prominence of the landscape — in Tintoretto's work, landscape is generally subordinate to the human figure. Most scholars date the work around 1550 when, perhaps

JACOPO TINTORETTO
St. George and the Dragon (circa 1550)
Canvas; 61 3/4" × 39".
Documentary sources refer to this work as an outstanding part of the Correr collection in Venice. Acquired through the Rev. W. Holwell Carr Bequest in 1831.

because of Titian's influence, Tintoretto was most interested in landscape. The composition is built up on a play of curved lines starting with the body of the kneeling princess. Her face is impassive but the tempestuous wind which has spread her mantle of pink silk puts her off-balance. The curve is repeated in the dead body, whose position has been interpreted as an allusion to the crucified Christ. A wider arc is described by the horseman and dragon, between the green woods and the walls of the fabulous city. Mysterious figures appear in the clouds, as in a sky imagined by Altdorfer. (A.P.)

PAOLO VERONESE. *Allegory of Love: Respect.*

It is not certain that the series to which this canvas belongs was painted for the Emperor Rudolph II, but the erotic theme unquestionably would have appealed to this sovereign, whose collection included many profane subjects with the allegorical and intellectual complications of Mannerism. The subject matter of these works has not been identified, but this painting is often called *Respect.* A young woman is shown asleep on a canopied bed covered with red-orange satin that emphasizes the delicate ivory of her skin. The position of her body, with the knee raised and the arms relaxed, brings out this chromatic counterpoint to the full. Against the background of the arch, seen from below and cutting across the blue sky,

PAOLO VERONESE
Verona 1528 — Venice 1588
Allegory of Love: Respect (circa 1570–75)
Canvas; 6'1 1/4" × 6'6 1/4".
One of a series of four paintings of allegories of love, all of which are in the National Gallery. They appear in the inventory of the Emperor Rudolph II's collection in Prague, which was compiled in 1637. After the sack of Prague, they entered the royal collection of Sweden, belonged to Queen Christina and subsequently to the Duke of Orléans. The National Gallery acquired them between 1890 and 1891.

is the figure of a soldier. His yellow costume creates a lively complementary effect. Cupid leads him toward the sleeping young woman. Judging from the perspective, the canvas must have been intended for a position high up on the wall of a room, rather than as a ceiling decoration. Veronese's religious paintings aroused the suspicions of the Inquisition; but here, in this profane subject, he was free to express his felicitous lyrical vein. (R.P.)

PAOLO VERONESE.   *Allegory of Love: Unfaithfulness.*
Sometimes called *Unfaithfulness* or the *Contest of Love,* this scene is part of the same series as *Respect.* The basic motif of the composition is the harmonious arc formed by the arms of the nude: it connects the young man dressed in red on the left and the soldier in the brownish corselet on the right. The whole group is set against a changeable gray-blue sky, and the leafy branches of the trees echo the main movement of the composition. Skillfully modeled in alabaster-like tonalities, the nude — supported compositionally by her mantle — is the dominant element in the work. Touches of light pick out her tresses, the hair ornament and the pearl necklace. All four paintings of the series (the other two are called *Happy Union* and *Scorn*) show Veronese's supreme ability to connect disparate elements in a single harmonious rhythm. Details of style and costume date the works between 1585 and 1590. (R.P.)

PAOLO VERONESE
Allegory of Love: Unfaithfulness (1575–80)
Canvas; 6'2 1/2" × 6'2 1/2".

GIOVANNI BATTISTA MORONI. *The Tailor.*

Moroni's best-known portrait, this work owes its fame not only to its high quality but also to the characterization of the subject. A seventeenth-century commentator, Boschini, emphasized the naturalness of the treatment. In Moroni's portraits of *The Lawyer* (National Gallery) and *The Magistrate* (Brescia, Pinacoteca Tasio Mertinengo), the subjects have been caught in attitudes typical of their professions, but this refined and melancholy young nobleman might have been portrayed with letters and rose petals. The range of color is discreet and has been executed in a soft impasto—having completely assimilated the early influence of Mannerism, Moroni expressed himself in the more muted tones common to the school of Brescia. (A.P.)

GIOVANNI BATTISTA MORONI
Albino circa 1529 — Bergamo 1578
The Tailor (1570)
Canvas; 38″ × 29″.
It belonged to the Grimani family in Venice in the late seventeenth century. In the nineteenth century, it was in the Federigo Frizzoni de Salis collection in Bergamo, from which it was acquired by the National Gallery in 1862.

PAOLO VERONESE. *St. Helen: Vision of the Cross.*

The composition, an unusual one for Veronese, is a free interpretation of an engraving derived from a drawing by Parmigianino (now in the Uffizi). The drawing in turn recalls Raphael in conception. Veronese, however, has transformed the structure of the work with his subtle but sumptuous palette, whose mellowness suggests a date late in his career. The low-keyed color intensifies the intimate feeling created by the figure of the saint, who is absorbed in peaceful meditation. (R.P.)

PAOLO VERONESE
St. Helen: Vision of the Cross (1570–75)
Canvas; 6′5 1/2″ × 3′9 1/4″.
In England by the beginning of the eighteenth century, it was purchased by the National Gallery in 1875.

LORENZO LOTTO. *A Lady as Lucretia.*

Lotto, who returned to Venice in 1526, was inevitably influenced by Titian. But the color range in this portrait, with its combination of gray, green and rust, still reflects the artist's earlier Bergamo period. The young woman's unstable pose recalls that of the figures in the *Annunciation* of Ponteranica, and her rather rustic gesture seems to contradict the lovingly painted refinements of her dress and coiffure. It is not likely, however, that Lotto intended to convey any irony in this picture of a strong-minded woman pointing to a drawing of Lucretia stabbing herself to defend her virtue. The Latin inscription on the piece of paper lying on the table says: "After Lucretia's example let no violated woman live." (A.P.)

LORENZO LOTTO
Venice circa 1480 — Loreto 1556
A Lady as Lucretia (circa 1528)
Canvas; 37 1/2″ × 43 1/4″.
First known in 1854 when, attributed to Giorgione, it was lent by Lord Southerk to the British Institution. Crowe and Cavalcaselle correctly ascribed it to Lotto in 1871. It was acquired by the Gallery in 1927.

SEBASTIANO DEL PIOMBO. *The Resurrection of Lazarus.*

SEBASTIANO DEL PIOMBO
Venice (?) circa 1485 — Rome 1547
The Resurrection of Lazarus (1517–19)
Panel transferred to canvas; 12′6″ × 9′5″.
Signed at bottom left: "SEBASTIANUS VE-
NETUS FACIE/BAT." Around 1715 it en-
tered the Orléans collection, was acquired by
Angerstein a century later, and then by the
National Gallery. In 1968 restoration and
cleaning revealed the brillance of its original
color relationships.

Cardinal Giulo de' Medici, the future Pope Clement VII, having been invested with the see of Narbonne, commissioned Raphael and Sebastiano del Piombo in 1516 to paint two large altarpieces for Narbonne Cathedral. Documents show that Sebastiano completed his painting by May 1, 1519 and that it was shipped to France in 1520. This important commission was undertaken in a tense atmosphere, because of the rivalry between the two artists. The tension, however, was stimulating for Sebastiano, who had left Raphael's orbit for the circle of Michelangelo — whose sculptural qualities and feeling for dramatic compositions were more congenial to him. Vasari suggests that Michelangelo collaborated in the work, at least providing the

CARAVAGGIO
(MICHELANGELO MERISI)
Caravaggio 1573 — Porto Ercole 1610
The Supper at Emmaus (1597)
Oil on canvas; 6'4 3/4" × 4'6 3/4".
Painted for the Mattei family in Rome, it then belonged to Scipione Borghese. Presented to the National Gallery by Lord Vernon in 1839.

Opposite, above: detail.

preliminary drawings. Many scholars accept this theory. The divergent main lines make for an unusual and striking composition. Most of the faces are probably portraits of contemporaries, and this element of reality keeps the painting from the generalization and abstraction that characterize Sebastiano's later work. The light that models the figures reveals a range of harsh colors outside the law of tonality. There is also a recollection of Venetian painting in the highly contrasted sky and the flashes of light in the landscape. (A.P.)

CARAVAGGIO. *The Supper at Emmaus.*

76 It is instructive to compare this early painting with a later version of the

same subject, now at the Brera, Milan. Here the movement and composition, derived from Leonardo's *Last Supper,* are imposed from the outside, and there seems to be a deliberate intention to reduce the religious subject to the level of an everyday encounter in a wine shop. This rather primitive realism makes the biblical theme seem worldly and naturalistic. In the Brera version, Caravaggio used the same technique to suggest greater truth, and tempered it with subtlety, disquietude and mystery. In this picture, though Caravaggio harks back to the fifteenth century and to Mannerism, he also anticipates his great contribution to seventeenth-century painting. Coming just after Veronese and Tintoretto, he heralds Rubens and Velázquez, both of whom were influenced by his art. (G.L.M.)

CANALETTO. *The Stonemason's Yard (Venice: Campo S. Vidal and S. Maria della Carità).*

This unusual theme attracted Canaletto because it offered the interesting contrast of the stones set against a familiar topographical view, as well as a record of the work being done for the façade of the neighboring church of S. Vidal. Today the view is very different. The campanile of S. Maria della Carità across the Grand Canal was removed in 1744; the building immediately to the right of the church was rebuilt with a white façade which is now the entrance to the Accademia; and a heavy wooden bridge called the Ponte dell'Accademia now spans the canal at a point on the left in the picture. Although this is an early work, it shows Canaletto's solid and acute perception of reality. During his trip to Rome in 1719 he probably

CANALETTO
(GIOVANNI ANTONIO CANAL)
Venice 1697 — Venice 1768
The Stonemason's Yard (Venice: Campo S. Vidal and S. Maria della Carità
(circa 1728–30)
Canvas; 48 1/2″ × 63 3/4″.
There is no documentation on this picture before 1808, when it was in Sir George Beaumont's collection, London. Acquired by the Gallery in the Sir George Beaumont Gift, 1823. In 1955, nineteenth-century repainting, especially in the sky, was removed.

acquired from local landscape painters the new idea of painting actual scenes rather than invented ones. The picture has an overall scenic effect; close study reveals innumerable delightful details of the Venetian environment. All are caught in the brilliant play of color, light, and shadow. (A.P.)

FRANCESCO GUARDI. *Venice: The Giudecca with the Zitelle.*

Guardi certainly painted this scene while on a boat. The painting was evidently intended to serve a double purpose: it depicts a typical Giudecca scene, showing the Palladian façade of the church of the Zitelle set solidly between the wings of the convent; and it also evokes the boat traffic of the basin, the slap of sails and the splashing of the oars. Extremely fine brushwork creates an atmospheric web of silvery color. (A.P.)

FRANCESCO GUARDI
Venice 1712 — Venice 1793
Venice: The Giudecca with the Zitelle
(1780–85)
Canvas; 7″ × 9″.
This little canvas and *Venice: The Punta della Dogana* were bequeathed by Mrs. Charles Carstairs in 1952. It had been bought in Venice by an English collector early in the nineteenth century.

GIOVANNI BATTISTA TIEPOLO. *The Trinity Appearing to St. Clement.*

This is a sketch for a larger work — the grandiose altarpiece for the Chapel of Our Lady at Nymphenburg which was consecrated in 1739 — commissioned by one of the major reformers of the early eighteenth century, the Prince Elector of Cologne, Clement August. The canvas is dated prior to 1739; in fact, its monumentality is in the spirit of the artist's work at the Gesuati in Venice between 1737 and 1739. There is no reason to suppose that there was a lapse of time between the "model" and the finished altarpiece. Aside from the ordinary differences between a sketch and a complete work, here there is a change in proportions: the altarpiece is exceptionally tall and narrow, which led Tiepolo to dramatize its composition, whereas in the sketch the composition is more relaxed, with some purely decorative elements. Against an irrationally monumental architectural background, the group of the Trinity and angels appears to the old Pontiff. He is an impressive figure wrapped in a gold mantle. The composition has been given a skillful rotary movement, for which the little angel with the insignia of the pope acts as the pivot. This magnificent painting, with its rich and luminous colors, must have fully satisfied the taste for triumphant religious effects that was so alive in Catholic Germany. (A.P.)

GIOVANNI BATTISTA TIEPOLO. *Rinaldo and the Magic Mirror* and *Seated Man and Girl with Vase.* p. 82

In the nineteenth century these two paintings were reunited with another pair showing Oriental couples. Undoubtedly, they all originally belonged to a much larger wall decoration, in which scenes with literary subjects alternated with purely decorative paintings. The canvases were probably executed around 1755, when Tiepolo painted a number of subjects connected with Torquato Tasso's epic poem, *Jerusalem Delivered. Rinaldo and the Magic Mirror,* the more substantial work of the two, shows the embarrassed Rinaldo wearing woman's clothes. It has the pleasing Tiepolesque palette shared by all four canvases; in addition, the brushwork has been utilized to build up the forms, adding a certain emotional intensity to the episode. (A.P.)

GIOVANNI BATTISTA TIEPOLO
Venice 1696 — Madrid 1770
The Trinity Appearing to St. Clement
(1736–37)
Canvas; 27 1/2″ × 22 1/2″.
The sketch for the large altarpiece now in the Alte Pinakothek, Munich. Probably it was among the pictures owned by the donor of the altarpiece, the Prince Elector Clement August, which were subsequently sold at Bonn in 1764. Acquired from an American private collection in 1957.

On page 82:
GIOVANNI BATTISTA TIEPOLO
Rinaldo and the Magic Mirror and *Seated Man and Girl with Vase* (circa 1755)
Canvas; 65″ × 21 1/4″.
In the Rosenberg sale in Vienna in 1883, the paintings were acquired in New York in 1960.

FLANDERS
HOLLAND

JAN VAN EYCK. *The Marriage of Giovanni Arnolfini and Giovanna Cenami.*

An outstanding work of the fifteenth century, this painting reflects the influences of French and Rhineland sculpture, Sienese color and light techiques, and European court art. But the linear and decorative aspects of these influences have been replaced by a seamless, living continuity, which is also evident in van Eyck's earlier portrait of Arnolfini (now in the Berlin-Dahlem Museum). In this double portrait, which is as solemn as an Annunciation, every element is included in a perspective system that has its vanishing point below the mirror. The intensity of visual truth invests each detail; the entire composition, in its limpid purity, creates a meaningful cosmos. Religious symbols abound in the picture: the rosary, the roundels on the frame of the mirror, and the post of the chair. The candle in the chandelier may be a nuptial symbol as well, and the little dog may represent Fidelity. Scholars have debated the symbolism and meaning of the work, but it is generally accepted that it shows a marriage scene, with the two witnesses (who would be standing where the spectator stands) appearing in the mirror. The Latin inscription on the wall — "Jan van Eyck was here, 1434" — seems to confirm that one of the figures may be a self-portrait.

JAN VAN EYCK. *Portrait of a Young Man.*

Painted two years earlier than the preceding work, this portrait may represent a musician. According to Panofsky, the half-Greek, half-Latin inscription of "TYMWΘEOC" refers to the ancient Greek musician Timotheus of Miletus and implies that the subject was a contemporary of van Eyck, perhaps Guillaume Dufay or Giles Binchois. The presence on the simulated stone parapet of the motto "LEAL SOVVENIR," which means "faithful remembrance," has not been satisfactorily explained. Compositionally, the figure has been set at a diagonal with respect to the rolled-up scroll in his hand. The movement is developed from right to left, with each passage of form subtly described by the limpid light. This creates the contemplative tension of the intelligent and sensitive face, which emerges from an almost nocturnal ground.

JAN VAN EYCK. *A Man in a Turban.*   *p. 86*

The subject of this portrait has not been identified but may have been the artist's father-in-law. The motto on the upper part of the frame appears in several of van Eyck's works. "AAC.IXH.XAN" is the archaic Flemish spelling of "as I can," and refers to the proverb: "As I can, not as I should like." The classical frame is an integral part of the work and serves as a

JAN VAN EYCK
Active circa 1422 — Bruges 1441
Portrait of a Young Man
Oil on panel; 13 1/4″ × 7 1/2″.
Signed and dated: October 10, 1432.
Acquired for the gallery from Karl Ross of Munich. On the back is a mysterious, unidentified elaborate marking. A copy painted on copper is in the Lochis collection of the gallery of Bergamo.

JAN VAN EYCK
The Marriage of Giovanni Arnolfini and Giovanna Cenami
Oil on panel; 32 1/4″ × 23 1/2″.
The coat of arms of Don Diego Guevara originally appeared on the frame. He gave it to Margaret of Austria, regent of Flanders. It was inherited by Mary of Hungary, who took it to Spain in 1556. The Alcazar inventories of 1700, 1754 and 1789 mention the painting. Subsequently it passed through the hands of a French general, Bélliard, and an English Major General, James Hay, who sold it to the Prince Regent for his collection at Carlton House in 1816–17.

86

window through which the light envelops the figure. Against the nocturnal infinity of the background, the subject in his red turban and fur-collared black garb looms forward imposingly. The noble and rather pensive face, with its aggressive expression, is deftly and surely drawn, as are the involutions of the turban.

ROGIER VAN DER WEYDEN. *Portrait of a Lady.*   *p. 87*
Although some critics consider this painting inferior in quality to other female portraits by van der Weyden, it clearly shows the artist's mastery of symmetrical form and composition, inspired by Ferrarese and Florentine art. Van der Weyden has maintained a coherent preference for subtly developed linear patterns. The pyramid of the hands — with the rings indicating the married status of the subject — is a variation on the larger pyramid formed by the entire figure: the solid volume of the head combines with filmy extensions of the headdress. Unlike in van Eyck's portraits, van der Weyden's subjects do not look at the spectator, but are withdrawn into their own refinement.

ROGIER VAN DER WEYDEN.   *The Magdalen Reading.*
A recent cleaning of this panel revealed the two figures, the cupboard and the window in the background. The panel is the right-hand fragment of an altarpiece that originally had a Madonna and Child with St. John the

ROGIER VAN DER WEYDEN
The Magdalen Reading
Panel; 24 1/4″ × 21 1/2″.
The painting has been transferred from its original wood backing to a mahogany panel. A fragment of an altarpiece, it and two other pieces were in the Narlus, Onne, Gulbenkian and Knoedler collections. It was acquired by the National Gallery from the Beaucousin collection in Paris in 1860.

Evangelist in the center, and two other figures on the left. The *Magdalen* in the Prado (attributed to Campin), which is dated 1438, clearly influenced van der Weyden. The artist followed the tradition of van Eyck in creating a spatial volume within which a play of light from both foreground and background produces a multiplicity of shadows and unexpected highlights. The continuous and complicated linear structures create visual surprise and convey a vivid emotional intensity.

ROBERT CAMPIN. *The Virgin and Child Before a Firescreen.*
Strips added to this work — the carved chest, the Virgin's elbow, and the area below the transom of the window — show later repainting. The left-hand side of the composition is missing, as indicated by the octagonal tile that marks the central axis of the pavement's perspective. Executed around 1430, when the artist was associated with van der Weyden, it shows the influence of that master. The firescreen, which also serves as the Virgin's halo, is derived from a miniature painting by the Limbourg brothers; Franco-Burgundian influence is seen also in the sumptuous plasticity of the drapery. Van Eyck's example is evident as well, in the multiple light sources and the limpid details. The Child, the book with its linen cover, and the upper part of the figure of the Virgin reveal an almost self-satisfied elaboration of linear patterns and structures.

ROBERT CAMPIN
The Virgin and Child before a Firescreen
Oak panel; 25″ × 19 1/4″.
Acquired in Venice in 1875 by Léon Somzée, this panel came to the National Gallery with the George Salting Bequest in 1910.
Above, right: detail of the window.

89

HANS MEMLING. *The Virgin and Child with Saints.*
The outer wings show St. John the Baptist on the left and St. John the
Evangelist on the right. In the center on a canopied throne sit the Virgin
and Child, surrounded by angels, and Saints Catherine and Barbara. Sir
John Donne, the donor of the triptych, kneels before the throne. He has
been identified by the coats of arms on the capitals of the columns supporting the loggia. His wife Elizabeth, in a purple gown, wears a Yorkist
collar and a medallion of Edward I. Memling included a portrait of
himself in the wing with St. John the Baptist. Memling's light graceful
touch combines Northern tradition with Italian influence to produce the
diffused brightness of the horizon and the rich countryside, and the melodic
play of lights and darks.

DIERIC BOUTS. *Portrait of a Man.*
This panel, probably the right-hand wing of a diptych, is the first securely
dated work by Bouts. Although the facts of Dieric Bouts' life and style are
still being debated by scholars, this portrait represents perhaps his most
limpidly intense period. In the sunny warmth and pensive serenity of this
portrait, he has achieved an exceptionally personal effect — though the
ideas derive from van Eyck and van der Weyden, while the composition
90 of form and volume derives from Italian art.

HANS MEMLING
The Virgin and Child with Saints
(*The Donne Triptych*) (1475–80)
Oil on panel; central panel, 28″ ×
26 3/4″, wings, 28″ × 11 3/4″.
On the reverse are simulated statues in gri-
saille of St. Christopher and St. Anthony
Abbot. From Lord Burlington of Chiswick
House, a descendant of the donors, the trip-
tych passed to the Dukes of Devonshire. It
was acquired by the National Gallery in
1956.

DIERIC BOUTS
Haarlem — Louvain 1475
Portrait of a Man (1462)
Oil on oak panel; 12 1/2″ × 8″.
This painting has been tentatively identified
with the so-called self-portrait of Rogier van
der Weyden which Marcantonio Michiel saw
in Venice in 1530. In 1831 it was in Karl
Aders' collection in London.

GERARD DAVID. *The Virgin and Child with Saints and Donor.*

The donor, kneeling on the left, has been securely identified from the coat of arms on his dog's collar as Richard de Visch de la Chapelle, cantor of St. Donatian's at Bruges. Very probably Bruges is the city glimpsed in the background. Painted between 1505 and 1510, the work shows a number of motifs taken from Memling, and handled with the exceptional simplicity typical of David's most accomplished works. The four majestic, self-absorbed figures placed around the delicate, traditional Virgin — St. Barbara, Mary Magdalen, St. Catherine and the donor — create a broad, semicircular space that is bathed in warm golden light. The stillness of the light and the hieratic figures create an atmosphere of ineffable peace and quiet.

GERARD DAVID
Oudewater — Bruges 1523
The Virgin and Child with Saints and Donor
Oil on oak panel; 41 3/4″ × 56 3/4″.
This panel is from the altar of St. Catherine in the church of St. Donatian, Bruges, where it remained until 1793. In the Edward Outran sale in Paris, 1877, and subsequently in the Lebrun and de Beurnonville collections, it was bequeathed to the National Gallery by Mrs. Lyne Stephens in 1895.

GERARD DAVID
Christ Nailed to the Cross
(circa 1480)
Oil on oak panel; 19″ × 37″.
A seal on the back refers to Our Lady of
Loreto. The wings of this small triptych
(now in Antwerp) bear the arms of Adolph
of Burgundy, the illegitimate grandson of
Philip the Good. Acquired by the Counts
of Thiene at Vicenza around 1850, it was
taken to England by Sir Austen Henri Layard, who bequeathed it to the National
Gallery in 1916.

GERARD DAVID. *Christ Nailed to the Cross.*
Although this panel is an early work, it is one of the most unusual and
original of David's career. The influence of Italian composition is obvious,
but the impetuous movement is new. The format consists of two squares;
the figure of Christ establishes a diagonal axis, and the composition moves
off in various directions established by his arms, the cloth and the other
figures. The isolated figures are given a triangular, monumental form that
breaks the rapid and dramatic main movement of the composition. David
seems to have freely adapted the little figures in the background from those
in the *Crucifixion* (Metropolitan Museum) by the brothers van Eyck.

HIERONYMUS BOSCH. *Christ Mocked.*

Bosch's many paintings of the Passion of Christ inspired numerous derivations and copies. This panel is one of his most outstanding works. The figures are composed on a system of diagonals that intensifies the impression of closeness created by the crowding of the foreground. Bosch has produced a grouping of grotesque and caricatural faces, whose cruelty and alienation contrast violently with the meek suffering of the sacred figure.

HIERONYMUS BOSCH
s' Hertogenbosch (?) 1450 —
s' Hertogenbosch 1516
Christ Mocked (circa 1480)
Oil on oak panel; 29″ × 23 1/4″.
The painting shows numerous corrections by the artist, especially in the hands and the upper part of Christ's robe. In the nineteenth century, it was in the Hollingworth Magniac collection at Colworth; it was bought for the Gallery in 1934.

94

PIETER BRUEGEL. *The Adoration of the Kings.*

This work, from the second half of Bruegel's brief career, represents a conscious return to the "primitive" Flemish tradition of van Eyck and Lucas van Leyden. Although there are references to Dürer and other Northern painters, the single most important influence is that of Bosch. The crossed diagonals of the composition center on the Christ Child. The old kings look like freebooters, and their rough soldier-retainers resemble the Spanish troops that were then occupying the Lowlands, while Joseph and the other bystanders are the familiar peasant types of Bruegel's repertory.

PETER PAUL RUBENS. *The Judgment of Paris.*

Rubens has treated the ancient myth of Paris with immediacy and realism — using his wife as the model for Aphrodite and familiar landscapes for the background. The shepherd Paris, with Hermes beside him, has decided that Aphrodite is the most beautiful of the three goddesses and is about to award her the prize of the golden apple. Eris, the personification of discord, is the figure that has appeared in the sky. The whole scene, which has the dash and lightness of a sketch, is drenched in a warm afternoon light. In richness and harmony the work shows Rubens' complete mastery of Baroque techniques of color, rhythm and composition.

PETER PAUL RUBENS. *The Castle of Steen.*

In this affectionate rendering of his own country house and lands, Rubens has given vitality to a landscape composed mainly of flat and uninteresting

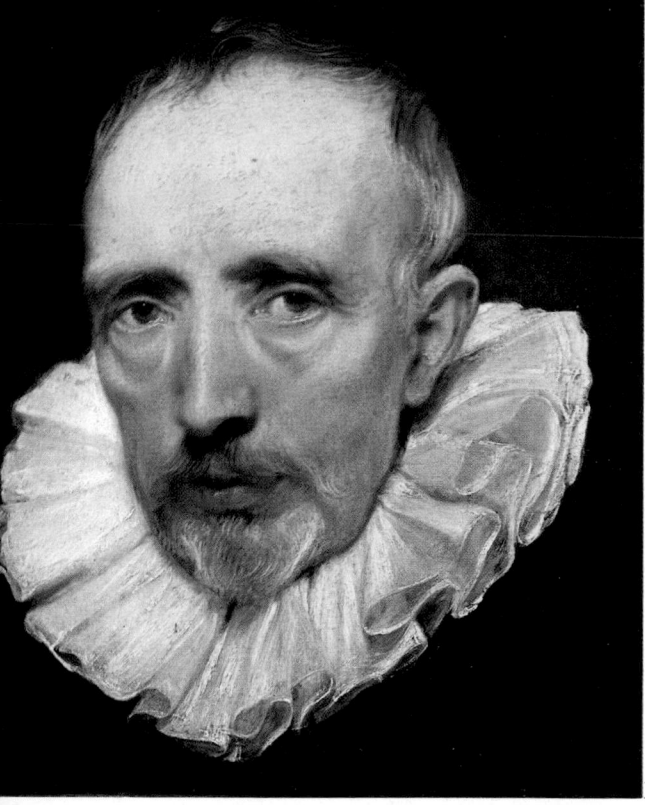

fields. It is a return to the type of landscape he favored in his youth; here, however, he does not represent the violence of nature but the quiet atmosphere of broad distances receding to the horizon in an afternoon light.

PETER PAUL RUBENS. *"Le Chapeau de Paille"* (*The Straw Hat*).
p. 97

The traditional title of this painting is confusing, since the woman's hat is not made of straw. One explanation is that the French word for straw *(paille)* is a corruption of "hair" *(poil)*. The subject may be Susanna Fourment, sister of Rubens' young second wife, Helena Fourment. It dates from the first year of his marriage (1630), and shows Rubens' command of every means of expressing youthful beauty and vitality. Combining brilliancy and subtlety, this is the only portrait of its time to show a sunlit figure in the open air.

ANTHONY VAN DYCK. *Cornelius van der Geest.*
Van Dyck considered this portrait one of his most successful, and it was included in the *Iconographia* — the series of one hundred of his great portraits published in Antwerp in 1646 by G. Hendricx. Painted before the artist was 20 years old, the portrait is a striking likeness of the subject — Cornelius van der Geest, an Antwerp merchant and art collector, who was a friend and patron of Rubens. Van der Geest's intelligence and sensitivity are reflected in a sumptuous and luminous painting that includes subtle touches and transparencies.

FRANS HALS. *Portrait of a Man Holding Gloves.*
Although the subject is unknown, he was a probably a citizen of Haarlem, where Hals did most of his work. The artist has reduced his palette to the few essential colors — mainly whites, blacks and grays — typical of his mature period. The figure is constructed with only a few simple planes that define the austere volumes. The fluid brushwork builds up the image with no attempt at finished, naturalistic description. The typical spare effect of the figure, the overall ground and the cast shadow anticipate the work of Velázquez.

REMBRANDT VAN RIJN. *The Woman Taken in Adultery.*
In this work from his early maturity, Rembrandt has developed a dramatic and choral theme. In a temple so vast that its roof and sides are lost in obscurity, two symphonically orchestrated but distinct actions take place:

in the background to the right is a glittering and sumptuous ceremony, revealed by the reflected lighting; in the foreground is the enactment of the parable from the Bible, spotlighted by a single beam from above. The group arranged in a semicircle around the adulteress stands out in a vivid light in the immense darkness and penumbra of the temple. This is an outstanding example of Rembrandt's fondness for theatrical effects, which can be seen in other paintings, etchings and drawings.

REMBRANDT VAN RIJN. *Self-Portrait at the Age of 34*.
This self-portrait is modeled on a sketch Rembrandt drew from memory of Raphael's *Portrait of Baldassar Castiglione*. Rembrandt incorporated the majestic construction and calm harmony of Raphael's painting into his own style. The theme of a figure lighted from the side and seen against a shadowy or intermittently lighted ground is in the tradition of Caravaggio. Within the strict discipline of the limited palette, the brushwork appears to send off unexpected flashes that express the inner vitality of the figure.

100

REMBRANDT VAN RIJN
Self-Portrait at the Age of 34
Canvas; 40 1/4" × 31 1/2".
Signed and dated 1640.
Bought by the National Gallery in 1861.

REMBRANDT VAN RIJN
Belshazzar's Feast
Oil on canvas; 5′5 3/4″ × 10′1 1/2″.
Signed and dated on the right. The last
figure of the date has been effaced.
The painting was in the 1736 catalog of the
Earl of Derby's collection at Knowsley Hall
from which it was acquired in 1964.

REMBRANDT VAN RIJN. *Belshazzar's Feast.*

The form of the Hebrew "handwriting on the wall," *Mene Mene Tekel Upharsin,* was suggested as the most authentic by Rembrandt's friend Mennaseh ben Israel, who also served as his model in 1636. With the *Blinding of Samson* in Frankfurt and the *Sacrifice of Isaac* in the Hermitage, this painting belongs to the period when the artist was most drawn to theatrical effects expressed in the powerful traction of opposing elements. Here the void at the right contrasts with the table advancing in the foreground; and the group at the left, receding toward the dark ground, counters the unstable pyramid made by the foreground group. A dazzling light beams from the celestial admonition, picking out the chromatic splendor of the rich costumes, jewelry and plate, as well as the emotional reactions of the group.

101

REMBRANDT VAN RIJN
Portrait of Margareta de Geer (circa 1661)
Oil on canvas; 51 1/4″ × 38 1/2″.
Portraits of Margareta and her husband were also painted by J. G. Cuyp and Nicolas Maes. This painting and its companion portrait were bought for the National Gallery in 1899.

Above, right:
REMBRANDT VAN RIJN
Portrait of the Painter in Old Age: In a Red Jacket with a Fur Collar, His Hands Clasped (circa 1660)
Oil on canvas; 33 3/4″ × 27 1/2″.
Bought for the Gallery in 1851.

REMBRANDT VAN RIJN
A Woman Bathing in a Stream
Oil on oak panel; 24 1/4″ × 18 1/2″.
Signed and dated 1654 (?).
From the Rev. W. Holwell Carr Bequest, 1831.

REMBRANDT VAN RIJN. *A Woman Bathing in a Stream.*
The model for this masterpiece was probably Hendrickje Stoffels, Rembrandt's common-law wife. Although the scarlet and gold robe on the bank suggests the biblical theme of Bathsheba, Rembrandt's concern is not a world of fantasy and history but rather the intimate feelings of a single human presence: a woman alone, finding her footing as she wades into a stream in the sunlight. This is a purely personal painting, executed for himself rather than for the market.

REMBRANDT VAN RIJN. *Portrait of Margareta de Geer.*
This painting forms a pair with Rembrandt's portrait of the subject's husband, Jacob Trip, also in the National Gallery. The Gallery also owns a half-length portrait of Margareta signed by Rembrandt and dated 1661. Against a ground troubled by densely falling shadows, the figure sits in a large armchair, with the opulent dress hiding the contours of her body. In this dusky atmosphere, Rembrandt has singled out the signs of bodily decay and expresses the subject's resignation as she patiently waits for death. The brilliant white starched collar throws into almost cruel relief the devastated face of the old woman; her veined and bony hands emerging from the rich fabric look like dried roots.

REMBRANDT VAN RIJN. *Portrait of the Painter in Old Age: In a Red Jacket with a Fur Collar, His Hands Clasped.* *p. 103*

This composition follows the Raphaelesque structural simplicity of the *Self-Portrait at the Age of 34,* but the figure has been brought forward to make a more immediate impact. The artist's face shows the effects of the sorrows and misfortunes that afflicted his old age. The atmosphere is dense and moving, with muffled flashes of light. In technique, the painting is summary and direct, and creates meaningful form by an infinity of vibrant touches and passages.

PIETER DE HOOCH. *A Woman and Her Maid in a Courtyard.*

A work of de Hooch's stylistic maturity, in theme this painting is related to the work of other seventeenth-century Dutch artists who focused on scenes of daily life. Simple forms are set against broad skies, and details are described with dispassionate serenity. A tranquil moment of mundane activity has been caught and transmuted into a timeless vision.

PIETER DE HOOCH. *An Interior with a Woman Drinking, with Two Men and a Maidservant.*

Warmth and conviviality are expressed in this simple domestic scene: one of the cavaliers reaches for the glass of wine the woman is holding, while the other raises his churchwarden pipe. A maid, carrying a pan, crosses toward them. The immaculate, prosperous interior, lighted by the radiance from the wall of windows, is reconstructed in impeccable perspective. Light, color and form are unified and share in the glowing warmth.

JAN VERMEER. *A Young Woman Standing at a Virginal.* *p. 106*

This painting and its companion, *A Young Woman Seated at a Virginal* (page 107), are generally dated in 1671, toward the end of the artist's brief career. They represent the consolidation of past achievements rather than the inspiration and innovations of many of Vermeer's earlier masterpieces. The composition is unsatisfactory, since the figure is crowded against chair, virginal (a musical instrument popular in the seventeenth century) and picture frame, and the relationship of the spectator to the picture as a whole is ambiguous. Nevertheless, the essential values of Vermeer's style are present: every element has a full three-dimensional form, the lyric quality of the light is sustained, and a mundane interior has been made into something

On page 106:
JAN VERMEER
Delft 1632 — Delft 1675
A Young Woman Standing at a Virginal
Oil on canvas; 20 1/4" × 16 1/2".
Signed on the virginal: *I Meer.*
Sold at auction in Amsterdam in 1797, then in various Parisian collections, the painting was purchased in 1892.

On page 107:
JAN VERMEER
A Young Woman Seated at a Virginal
Oil on canvas; 20 1/4" × 17 3/4".
George Salting Bequest, 1910.

PIETER DE HOOCH
Delft 1629 — Amsterdam circa 1684
A Woman and Her Maid in a Courtyard
Oil on canvas; 29″ × 24 1/2″.
Inscribed: P.D.H. 166–.
Bought for the Gallery in 1869.

PIETER DE HOOCH
*An Interior with a Woman Drinking, with
Two Men and a Maidservant*
Oil on canvas; 29″ × 25 1/2″.
It bears the inscription: P.D.H.
Bought in 1871.

sublime. Most likely, Vermeer invented the landscape painted on the lid of the virginal. The painting of *Cupid* on the wall — which also appears in *Sleeping Girl* (Metropolitan Museum) and in *Duet* (Frick Collection) — has been attributed to Cesar van Everdingen and Jan van Bronckhorst.

JAN VERMEER. *A Young Woman Seated at a Virginal.* p. 107
The painting hanging on the wall in the background, which also appears in *The Concert* in the Gardner Collection, Boston, is *The Procuress* by Theodor van Baburen; the original belonged to Vermeer. The virginal is very similar to the one represented in *A Young Woman Standing at a Virginal,* but there are some differences in the landscape painted on the lid. The instrument has been identified as one produced by the Ruckers factory in Antwerp. Iconographically, the player derives from a popular type of St. Cecilia which had been adapted for portraiture by Dirk Hals and Jan Miense Molenaer.

JACOB VAN RUISDAEL. *The Shore at Egmond-aan-Zee.*
Following the tradition of seventeenth-century Dutch landscape painting,
Ruisdael based this picture on an underlying system of regular proportions. Simple divisions are eminently applicable to the flat plains, low hori-
zons and towering skies of the Netherlandish countryside. Ruisdael's dramatic imagination is seen here in the time of day: twilight approaches and
a single ray of sunshine rakes the foreground. Sky and water blend, as
real and reflected clouds echo one another. Objects and their reflections
maintain a precarious equilibrium.

108

JACOB VAN RUISDAEL
Haarlem circa 1628 — Amsterdam (?) 1682
The Shore at Egmond-aan-Zee
Oil on canvas; 21″ × 26″.
Inscribed: JvRuisdael (JvR in monogram).
Bought for the Gallery in 1893.

CAREL FABRITIUS. *A View in Delft, With a Musical Instrument Seller's Stall.*

CAREL FABRITIUS
Midden-Beemster 1622 — Delft 1654
*A View in Delft, With a Musical
Instrument Seller's Stall*
Oil on canvas, transferred to wood;
6″ × 12 1/2″.
Signed and dated: C. Fabritius 1652.
Presented by the National Art-Collections
Fund, 1922.

Fabritius' highly personal imagination is exemplified in this painting, dated two years before his death. Two separate views are counterposed here. On the left there is a quiet genre scene, with shadows gathering in an evening light; to the right, beyond the tree, is a broad panorama that stretches out in full, radiant daylight. The effect of the whole composition is meditative, visionary and original.

109

GERARD TER BORCH. *A Young Woman Playing a Theorbo to Two Men.*

Although appreciated for depicting seventeenth-century Dutch customs and surroundings, the painters of interiors were not generally credited with great artistic qualities. A work such as this little painting, with its warm and subtle intimacy, belies such a view. Casual though it seems, the composition is carefully laid out on an underlying structure. The luminous atmosphere and the measured harmony of the tones create a cordial and pleasing effect.

110

GERARD TER BORCH
Zwolle 1617 — Deventer 1681
A Young Woman Playing a Theorbo to Two Men
Oil on canvas; 26 3/4″ × 22 3/4″.
Bought for the National Gallery in 1871.

JAN STEEN
Leiden 1626 — Leiden 1679
Skittle Players Outside an Inn
Oil on oak panel; 13 1/4″ × 10 3/4″.
George Salting Bequest, 1910.

JAN STEEN. *Skittle Players Outside an Inn.*
Steen seems to have composed this early work spontaneously, though with
a firm framework at his fingertips. The activity of the game of skittles
and other incidents below are balanced above by a multiplicity of green and
silvery leaves. The entire picture is bathed in a cheerful springtime light.

111

MEINDERT HOBBEMA. *The Avenue, Middelharnis.*

This last of the great seventeenth-century Dutch landscapes is more invented than real. The artist sketched from nature but composed in the studio according to strict systems of construction. In Hobbema's painting, geometry plays a fundamental role. In this three-part composition, the deep perspective made by the trees, and the contrasts and harmonies of the lateral movements, are outstanding. Hobbema created a permanent and monumental vision from transient and evanescent effects.

112

MEINDERT HOBBEMA
Amsterdam 1638 — Amsterdam 1709
The Avenue, Middelharnis
Oil on canvas; 40 3/4" × 55 1/2".
Inscribed: M:hobbema / f 1689.
Middelharnis is on the island of Over Flakee
in southern Holland.
Bought in 1871 for the National Gallery.

GERMANY

MASTER OF THE LIFE OF THE VIRGIN. *The Conversion of St. Hubert.*

With *The Mass of St. Hubert* and two other panels (all in the National Gallery), this painting was part of an altarpiece formerly in the Abbey of Werden (Düsseldorf). First ascribed to an unknown artist designated as the Master of Werden, these paintings are now attributed to a Cologne painter known as the Master of the Life of the Virgin. The artist has the dreamlike quality and brilliant color effects of Lochner and the Cologne School. This derivation is apparent also in the representation of the saints and in the heraldic linear rhythms and details. In this scene, the anonymous artist was inspired by contemporary Flemish works, such as Dieric Bouts'. He has created a new image while following traditional iconography. The apparition was motivated by the fact that Hubert was hunting during Holy Week. Reproved for this sin, he subsequently entered the Church and became the patron saint of hunters. He is shown here as an elegant courtly figure, contrasting with the airy rural climate of the broad landscape and the wooded hills receding to the blue distance and the golden sky.

LUCAS CRANACH. *Jealousy.* *p. 116*

In this magnificent painting, hooked rocks of impossible shape, pointed crockets and thorny scrub create an audacious landscape against the clear sky above. The foreground is limited by the screen of dark foliage, enlivened by golden glints, which forms a finely worked tapestry. Arranged in various attitudes and positions, the little nudes also make a pattern of contrasting rhythms and sinuous cadences. The figures rotating around the woman in the center create an intricate but controlled composition whose movement is underscored by the positions of the clubs. Cranach's qualities are so individual that it is often difficult to discover a specific mythological subject in his work.

LUCAS CRANACH. *Venus and Cupid.* *p. 117*

Cranach painted many versions of this subject, taken from the 19th Idyll of Theocritus: Cupid complains to Venus that he was stung by bees while stealing a honeycomb. The oldest existing version dates from 1529, and the present panel is very close to it in style. The two moralizing Latin couplets inscribed on the panel, which point out that pain follows pleasure, have no connection with Theocritus. Except for the theme, the composition owes more to the Middle Ages than to Greco-Roman culture, as can be seen in the geometrical distribution of the underlying structure. The main element is the female nude, who moves with serpentine fluency across the surface, negating weight and substance with her undulations reflected in the pulsating lights and darks. The thick shady foliage, the rough cracked bark of the tree trunk, and the fruit-laden branches provide an accompaniment to the capricious, dancing figure.

ALBRECHT DÜRER
Nuremberg 1471 — Nuremberg 1528
The Painter's Father
Limewood panel; 20″ × 15 3/4″.
The German inscription states: "1497 Albrecht Dürer the Elder, 70 years old." This is the best of four versions by the artist (the others are in the museums of Frankfurt and Erlangen and in the Duke of Northumberland's collection at Syon House). The painting was given to Charles I by the city of Nuremberg. Subsequently it belonged to Lady Ashburton and then to the Marquis of Northampton, who sold it to the Gallery in 1904. Cleaning in 1955 revealed major retouching that had covered up innumerable little cracks caused by the expansion and contraction of the panel.

ALBRECHT DÜRER. *The Painter's Father.*

Some critics erroneously take this painting to be a replica of a lost original or of the portrait of the artist's father in the Uffizi, which was executed in 1490. Dürer's father, a goldsmith, was born in Hungary but settled in the free city of Nuremberg. While still a boy, young Albrecht was apprenticed to the painter Michael Wolgemut, who had been influenced by Flemish art. Dürer was 26 when he painted this portrait, which shows Flemish and Italian influence in the pyramidal composition, the balance of the masses around a central core and the architectonic relationship of arms, body, shoulders and head. In this imperiously simple and imposing structure, the artist has subtly incorporated asymmetrical passages and unexpected changes of direction that animate the otherwise static figure. These details are most evident in the bony development of the head, the wrinkles and the serpentine locks.

ALBRECHT ALTDORFER
Ratisbon (?) circa 1480 — Ratisbon 1538
Landscape With a Footbridge
Oil on parchment on panel; 16 1/2″ × 14″.
Signed with the monogram "A A" on the right. It was acquired from J. Koerfer of Berne in 1961.

ALBRECHT ALTDORFER. *Landscape With a Footbridge.* *p. 119*
This painting is one of the first known "pure" landscapes. In style, it shows the influence of Giorgione and Venetian painting, though it is certain that Altdorfer never went to Venice. Particularly reminiscent of Giorgione are the background under the bridge and the rosy dawn sky. The pure fantasy in this landscape shows a mysterious influence from Far Eastern painting, especially in the wooden bridge and the branches erupting in the sky with the verticality typical of Chinese and Japanese landscapes.

HANS HOLBEIN THE YOUNGER. *Jean de Dinteville and Georges de Selve ("The Ambassadors").*
Jean de Dinteville, French Ambassador to England, is on the left. His friend, Bishop Georges de Selve, on the right, served as ambassador to the Emperor, the city of Venice and the Pope. On the lower shelf is a German Protestant hymn book, open to two Lutheran hymns. This unusual element in a painting of two Catholic diplomats is explained by the fact that de Selve sympathized with the Reformation. This large, imposing and somewhat hieratic double portrait is an extraordinary compendium of geometry and perspective in pictorial representation. The geometric pattern of the mosaic pavement, copied from fourteenth-century Cosmatesque work in Westminster Abbey, defines the plane on which the figures and the shelves stand. Objects of complicated shape — the lute, the astronomical and chronological instruments — are depicted with virtuosity. The anamorphic skull — which seems to be an unidentifiable object suspended in space, until viewed from the side — is a visual game.

HANS HOLBEIN THE YOUNGER
Augsburg 1497 — London 1543
Jean de Dinteville and Georges de Selve ("The Ambassadors")
Oil and tempera on panel;
6′9 1/2″ × 6′10 1/2″.
Signed and dated 1533.
Taken to France by de Dinteville, it was sold by his descendants in 1787 to the dealer J. B. P. Lebrun. It then entered the collection of the Earls of Radnor at Longford Castle, and was bought for the Gallery in 1890.

HANS HOLBEIN THE YOUNGER. *Christina of Denmark, Duchess of Milan.* *p. 122*
Holbein was sent by Henry VIII in 1538 to negotiate a marriage between the king and Christina of Denmark. He did her portrait (in three hours, it was reported) but the marriage did not take place. (The painting was probably made in London from the life sketch.) The magnificent widow in her silky black velvet gown is set against an even ground broken only by cast shadows. Although there are no indications of movement, she seems

to have been caught off-guard. All extraneous detail has been eliminated, so that there are no distractions to diminish the imposing singleness of the vision. The picture is built up on a few simple planes and has a limited color range; the figure is fundamentally made up of a cone crowned by the circular disposition of the head, arms and hands.

122

HANS HOLBEIN THE YOUNGER
Christina of Denmark, Duchess of Milan
Oil and tempera on panel;
70 1/2" × 32 1/2".
This painting was made by the artist in his London studio from a life sketch. The sketch itself has been lost; the small half-length sketch at Windsor Castle is apparently a copy.
Acquired in 1909 from the Howard family.

FRANCE

FRENCH ARTIST OF THE 14TH CENTURY. *Richard II Presented to the Virgin and Child by His Patron Saints ("The Wilton Diptych").* pp. 124–125

Probably painted to support dynastic claims, this unique diptych of Richard II, King of England, has been claimed both as a French and an English work. Various hypotheses have been advanced as to its date: 1395, for the king's marriage to Isabel of France; 1401 or before 1406, if commissioned in France by his widow; 1413, for the king's burial at Westminster. Since it owes much to Sienese art, the painting is probably the work of a Frenchman or an artist educated in France. It is also connected with the style of miniature painters like Beauneveu and Hermann Scheere. The patron saints are John the Baptist, Edmund, last King of East Anglia, and Edward the Confessor. The angels wear the French collar and the English badge. In its delicately musical rhythms and springtime colors, the diptych is one of the major paintings prior to the brothers van Eyck.

MASTER OF ST. GILES. *St. Giles and the Hind.*

Only a few other works by this artist are known: *The Mass of St. Giles* (National Gallery) and two scenes from the *Life of St. Remigius* (National Gallery of Washington). This panel was probably the central part of a triptych. It shows the misadventure of St. Giles, a hermit of Provence, whose only companion was a hind. The king, out hunting, aimed an arrow at the beast but hit the holy man in the hand instead. In this scene, the king, accompanied by a bishop, has come to ask forgiveness. The town in the background may be Saint-Gilles-du-Gard, near Arles. The artist probably was active in northern France around 1500, and had a Flemish education. Various influences including those of David, Geertgen tot Sint Jans, Josse Liefrinxe and Hugo van der Goes can be discerned. Italian techniques of composition are reflected in the central columnar tree — around which the main figures are arranged cubically, while the others are disposed along diagonals. This arrangement permits a ready recession of the space toward the distant background landscape.

NICOLAS POUSSIN. *Bacchanalian Revel Before a Term of Pan. p. 128*

Some scholars think this painting was one of the *Bacchanals* executed for Cardinal Richelieu around 1635, but there is no concrete evidence for this view. The entire composition is developed on the oblique. Movement on the surface and in depth has its focal point in the fallen nymph in the right foreground. An opposite movement is created by the mass of trees, starting from the right and stopping, like the figures below, to reveal the luminous expanse of plains, distant mountains and sky. The precisely con-

On pages 124–125:
FRENCH ARTIST OF THE
14TH CENTURY
Richard II Presented to the Virgin and Child by His Patron Saints ("The Wilton Diptych")
Panel; 18″ × 11 1/2″ (with
original frame 21″ × 14 1/2″).
On the reverse of the panels, a white hart on the right is Richard II's emblem; on the left are the arms of Edward the Confessor.
From the collection of King Charles I, it passed to the Earls of Pembroke at Wilton House, and was bought for the Gallery in 1929.

MASTER OF ST. GILES
Active in northern France circa 1500
St. Giles and the Hind
Panel; 24 1/4″ × 18 1/4″.
On the reverse is a bishop in a niche in grisaille.
Bought from the Earl of Northbrook in 1894.

structed "scissors" composition is veiled, however, by the warmly sensuous colors and the sinuous elegance of the motifs. X-ray examination has shown that the painting was executed on top of a completely different earlier version in which the composition is reversed and the figures are larger.

CLAUDE LORRAINE. *Landscape: The Marriage of Isaac and Rebekah ("The Mill").*

With its companion piece, *Seaport: Embarkation of the Queen of Sheba,* this painting was executed by Claude in 1648. Other versions are in the national museum in Budapest and in the Doria Pamphili collection, Rome. As with Claude's other works, the composition follows a very simple

NICOLAS POUSSIN
Les Andelys 1594 — Rome 1665
Bacchanalian Revel Before a Term of Pan
Oil on canvas; 39 1/4″ × 56″.
The painting passed from numerous private English collections to the National Gallery in 1826. Other copies exist, and it has been engraved many times.

CLAUDE LORRAINE
Champagne 1600 — Rome 1682
*Landscape: The Marriage of Isaac and
Rebekah ("The Mill")*
Oil on canvas; 4'10 3/4" × 6'5 1/2".
The title is inscribed on a tree trunk in the
center. Signed and dated 1648 below. Commissioned by Camillo Pamphili in 1647, it
was sold instead to the Duc de Bouillon, who
in turn sold it to Fitzinger. Subsequently it
belonged to the Angerstein collection, from
which it was acquired by the National Gallery in 1824.

scheme. Like the sweep of a compass, the movement swings from the
"wing" of trees on the right to the opposite grove. From the waterfall and
the distant bridge, two new directions of movements are created which
involve the entire luminous spread of the horizon. The figures do not
hamper the recession of the space, from the broad shaded foreground to
the infinite sea of noonday light.

LOUIS LE NAIN. *The Adoration of the Shepherds.* p. 130
Before 1962, when it came to the gallery, this painting was incorrectly
attributed to Luca Giordano. In a more or less correctly classical setting, **129**

which makes its effect through the silvery tones of the buildings and the pale blue sky, the simple everyday scene has been composed in a star shape around the Christ Child. In general orientation, Le Nain derives from Caravaggio, with Gentileschi as the intermediary. There is also some influence from Bassano and the Venetians. Warm, human and intimate in atmosphere, the painting makes no concession to ritual or religious rhetoric.

PHILLIPPE DE CHAMPAIGNE.   *Triple Portrait of Richelieu.*
Cardinal Richelieu, chief minister of France, wears the Order of the Holy Ghost in this triple portrait. The inscription in French over the profile on the right says: "This one is the better of the two profiles." Another inscription on the back of the canvas states that the triple portrait was sent to Francesco Mochi in Rome, who sculpted a bust from it, which he then shipped to Paris. The portrait reveals much more than a likeness of

LOUIS LE NAIN
Laon circa 1593 — Paris 1648
The Adoration of the Shepherds
Oil on canvas; 43″ × 54″.
Acquired from the collection of the Duke of Norfolk in 1962.

the subject; it carries personal characterization almost to the point of irreverence. This interior vision in scarlet, white and gold, which expresses the artist's skill and originality, seems suffused with the Cardinal's Machiavellian energy.

ANTOINE WATTEAU. *"La Gamme d'Amour"* (*The Gamut of Love*).
p. 132

This luminous painting stands out in particular for its composition, which involves multiple movements in depth and on the surface. There is a double recession in depth toward the luminous distance and in the diagonal disposition of the main group. The figures show an alternation — without weight or stability — of forms, carrying the play of color that helps to create the almost phosphorescent atmosphere. Although critics do not agree

131

on the meaning of the figures placed in the hollow among the trees on the right, they are participants in the warm idyllic scene, benevolently presided over by a pillar with the head of Pan.

JEAN-BAPTISTE SIMÉON CHARDIN. *The Young School Mistress.* Chardin returned frequently to this subject, subtly varying the relationships of form and color. The theme may be casual — a scene from everyday life

ANTOINE WATTEAU
Valenciennes 1684 — Valenciennes 1721
"La Gamme d'Amour"
(*The Gamut of Love*) (circa 1717)
Oil on canvas; 20″ × 23 1/2″.
A number of engravings were made from this painting, and there are many free interpretations by Pater. Numerous preliminary drawings exist in various museums and collections. After leaving the Denys Mariette collection the painting changed hands frequently before its acquisition by Sir Julius Wernher, who bequeathed it to the Gallery in 1912.

JEAN-BAPTISTE SIMÉON CHARDIN
Paris 1699 — Paris 1779
The Young School Mistress
Oil on canvas; 24 1/4″ × 26 1/4″.
Signed: "chardin."
The painting was exhibited at the 1740 Salon.
Seven versions are known, including an ex-
cellent one in Dublin and another in the
National Gallery of Washington. Acquired
with the John Webb Bequest, 1925.

such as the Dutch might have painted — but its development is concentrated and analytic. The two figures and the desk are treated like pieces of
sculpture. There is no edge or contour that does not turn the eye back into
depth, and the three-dimensional forms are carefully interrelated so that
their volumes appear to be set in ample space. Color and light are the means
of establishing these qualities and the overall unity of the work.

133

JEAN AUGUSTE DOMINIQUE INGRES
Montauban 1780 — Paris 1867
Madame Moitessier Seated
Oil on canvas; 47 1/4″ × 36 1/4″.
In the upper right corner, Ingres inscribed
the name of the subject: Mme. Ines Moitessier, née de Foucauld. On the mirror frame,
he signed his name and the date 1865, also
giving his age as 76.
A sketch for this portrait is in the museum
of Montauban. Some corrections are evident
in the sofa and the right arm. It was acquired
from a descendant of the model, the Vicomtesse de Bondy, in 1936.

JEAN AUGUSTE DOMINIQUE INGRES. *Madame Moitessier Seated.*
Begun in 1845, this portrait underwent various changes before Ingres completed it twelve years later. When the poet Théophile Gautier saw it in 1847, the subject's little daughter Catherine was at her mother's knee. In the final version, the figure of the daughter was eliminated. The subject's seated pose is derived from a Roman wall painting, the *Herakles and Telephus* from Herculaneum, now in the Naples Museum. The triumphant, monumental effect of the self-assured woman is created not only by the classical pose, but also by the doubling of the space in the reflection of the broad mirror and by the flawlessly smooth painting of skin and textures. Ingres owed much to Raphael, but both he and the Renaissance painter were looking back toward antiquity.

EUGÈNE DELACROIX. *Portrait of Baron Schwiter.* *p. 136*
In this portrait of a fellow painter, Delacroix broke with classical polish and used more intense colors than was customary among his contemporaries. Lawrence may have influenced the general composition and approach. The work apparently looked too unprofessional to be accepted for the 1827 Salon; after this rejection, Delacroix made some changes, especially on the parapet, and only completed the picture definitively in 1830. According to Moreau, the landscape was in part painted by Paul Huet, who had been Delacroix' fellow student in the studio of Guérin. A well-known landscape painter, Huet was a follower of the English landscapists, Bonington and Constable. The subject, Baron Louis Auguste Schwiter, was himself a landscape and portrait painter; thus the portrait was probably not a commissioned work but a mark of friendship between the two men.

HONORÉ DAUMIER. *Don Quixote and Sancho Panza.* *p. 137*
Cervantes' heroes appealed to Daumier's spirit — in which bitterness, disillusion and disdain conflicted with his conviction that life must inevitably become more enlightened. The literary masterpiece, with its irony and its indomitable belief in dreams and ideals, struck a sympathetic chord in the artist. Drawing inspiration from Rembrandt and Goya, Daumier concentrated the image by setting it against the light. Every element is shown in strong contrast and relief. In a dazzling, desert plain, under a pitiless sky, the shapes stand out as luminous surging forms among the tormented, receding shadows.

EUGENE DELACROIX
Charenton-Saint-Maurice 1798 — Paris 1863
Portrait of Baron Schwiter
Oil on canvas; 7'1 1/4" × 4'8 1/4".
After the death of the subject, the painting
was sold at auction in 1890. It belonged to
Degas, and was bought at his sale in 1918.

GUSTAVE COURBET.   *Still Life: Apples and Pomegranates.*
Although still lifes had been popularized by the Dutch painters, Courbet took Chardin, rather than the Dutch, as his model. Compact, solid, tangible and simple, the work has the air of direct realism on which the artist prided himself. The textures are bold and coarse, the colors earthy. Chardin's subtleties and complexities are reduced to something elemental and direct, but the grasp of form is masterful. The date next to the signature is 1871, the year of Courbet's imprisonment. During the short-lived Commune after the collapse of Napoleon III's empire, Courbet was elected president of the artists' federation and was present when the column in Place Vendôme, which had been erected by Napoleon I, was pulled down. Under the new regime he was arrested and forced to pay for restoring the column. In 1873 he fled France and died four years later in exile in Switzerland.

EDOUARD MANET.   *The Waitress ("La Servante de Bocks"). p. 138*
In 1878 Manet started on a large, ambitious canvas which he subsequently cut in two. The present work was the right-hand part of the larger composition; the left-hand part, *At the Cafe,* is in the Reinhart collection. The original painting had been rather statically balanced, which did not suit the vibrant, discontinuous brushwork and color. The two separate parts of the picture were considerably changed by the artist; they took on the immediacy of snapshots. The model is a waitress from a cafe Manet frequented in the Boulevard Rochechouart, Reichshofen's *Cafe-Concert.* She agreed to pose for the artist in his studio only if she could bring along a chaperon — he appears in the painting as the man smoking a pipe in the foreground.

EDOUARD MANET.   *Eva Gonzalès.*   *p. 139*
Manet began this portrait of his only pupil a few days after she started to work in his studio. According to a letter written by Berthe Morisot at the time, forty sessions went into the painting and then Manet wiped it out before going on to complete it on March 12, 1870, the last day he could enter it for that year's Salon. Although his inspiration was still from Velázquez, Manet achieved a new departure rather than a continuation of tradition. In composition, the work is anchored to three main axes, which are established by the flower and the scroll, the body of the figure and the

Opposite, above:
HONORÉ DAUMIER
Marseilles 1808 — Paris 1870
Don Quixote and Sancho Panza
Oil on panel; 16" × 25 1/4".
This is an unfinished sketch for the larger completed version in the Shipman Payson collection. A variant of the same subject is in the Berlin-Dahlem museum. In the Sir Hugh Lane Bequest of 1917, it was given to the Tate Gallery, from which it was transferred to the National Gallery in 1956.

Opposite, below:
GUSTAVE COURBET
Ornans 1819 — La Tour-de-Peilz 1877
Still Life: Apples and Pomegranates
Oil on canvas; 17 1/2" × 24".
Signed and dated: "G. Courbet 71."
Originally larger, the canvas was cut down on the right and above, and some of the painting is folded over the stretcher.
Acquired in 1951 from Arthur Tooth.

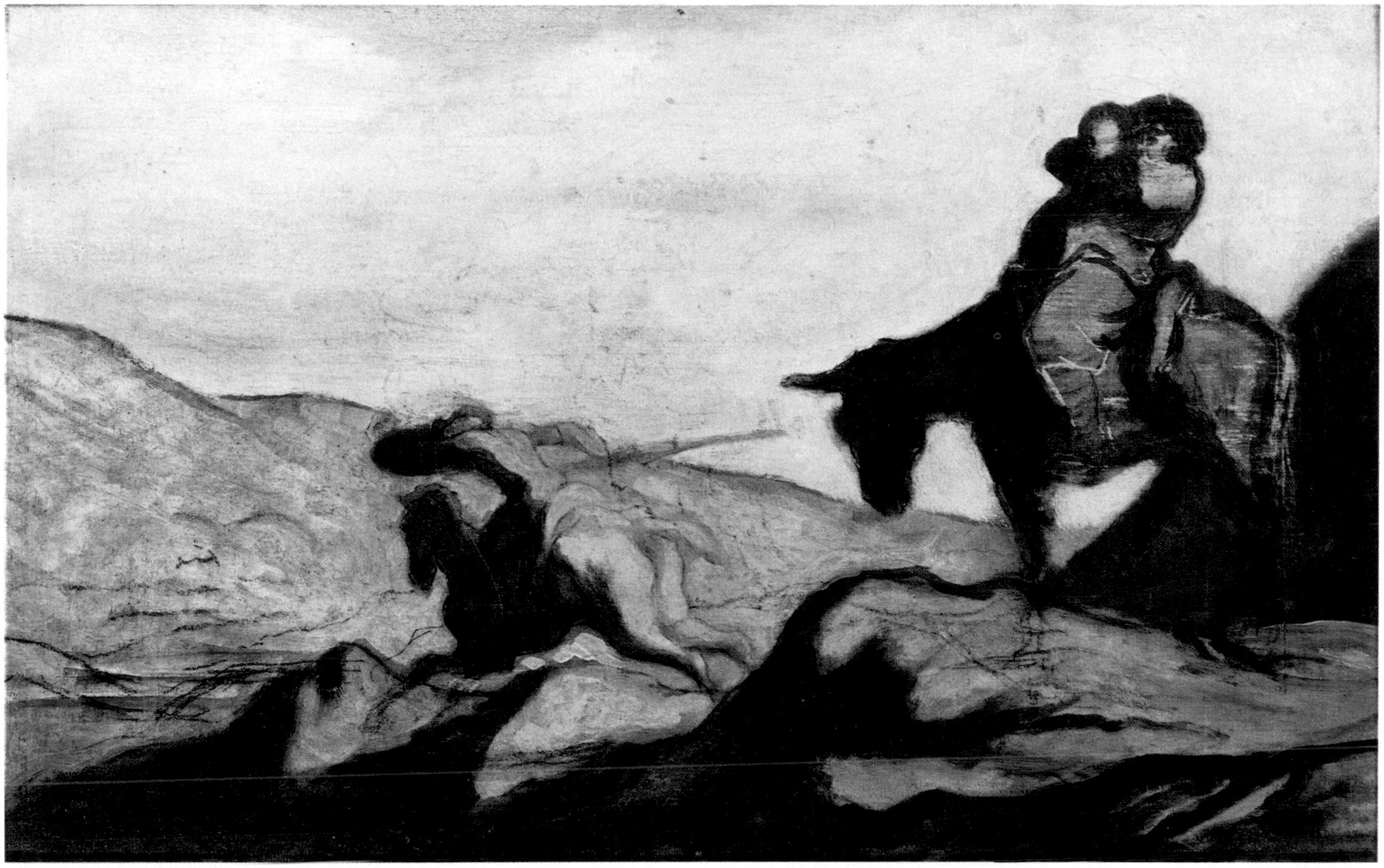

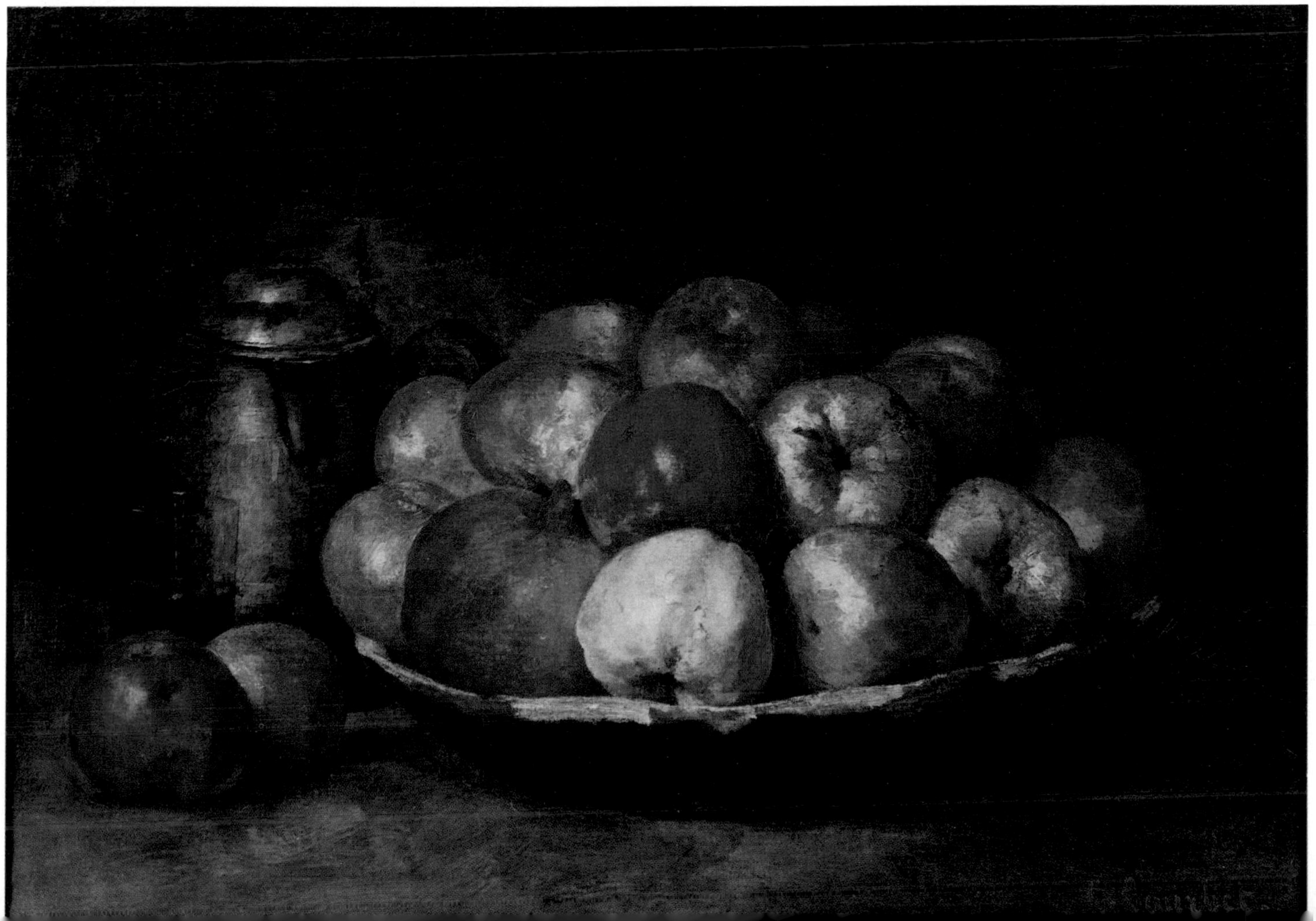

EDOUARD MANET
Eva Gonzalès
Oil on canvas: 6′3 1/4″ × 4′4 1/4″.
Signed: "manet 1870."
Some corrections have been made, especially in the chair. Given to the sitter by Manet, it became the property of her husband, the engraver Henri Guérin. Subsequently it was in the Durand-Ruel collection. It went to the Tate Gallery with the Sir Hugh Lane Bequest in 1917, and was transferred to the National Gallery in 1950.

EDOUARD MANET
Paris 1832 — Paris 1883
The Waitress ("La Servante de Bocks")
Oil on canvas; 38 1/2″ × 30 1/2″.
Donated to the Tate Gallery in 1924, the painting was transferred to the National Gallery in 1952.

chair, and the figure's elbow. Beyond this are the livelier episodes of the head, the arm in motion and the still life on the easel. A dominant note is the sparkling passage of the trailing white dress.

139

EDGAR DEGAS. *Combing the Hair.*

Degas took his subjects from contemporary life. This unfinished picture is one of many drawings, pastels and oil paintings that he devoted to the same subject over a period of ten years. It appealed to him because he could readily combine a clear, firm composition and a suggestion of action expressed in vibrant color and light. Accordingly, the design is steeply diagonal, from the table to the background; and in the space between, the figures perform the coordinated, choreographic gestures of their momentary activity. The artist suspended or interrupted this painting at the points where further definition would have vitiated the force of the scene.

PAUL CÉZANNE. *"Les Grandes Baigneuses"* (*The Large Bathers*).

In the last ten years of his life Cézanne painted three large versions of this subject. The other two, which are bigger, are now in the Barnes Foundation at Merion, Pennsylvania, and in the Philadelphia Museum. Alterations in the dimensions and in the color show that this canvas was painted after the Philadelphia version. The conclusion is borne out also by the unity

EDGAR DEGAS
Paris 1834 — Paris 1917
Combing the Hair
Oil on canvas; 45″ × 57 1/2″.
This is generally considered a later reworking (circa 1892–95) of earlier versions painted in 1885. Bought at the first Degas sale in 1918 by Henri Matisse, it then belonged to his son Pierre. Acquired by the Gallery in 1937.

PAUL CÉZANNE
Aix-en-Provence 1839 —
Aix-en-Provence 1906
"Les Grandes Baigneuses"
(The Large Bathers)
Oil on canvas; 4'2" × 6'5 1/4".
It was bought by the National Gallery in
1964 from the collection of Mme. Lecomte,
daughter of Auguste Pellerin.

AUGUSTE RENOIR
Limoges 1841 — Cagnes 1919
Dancer with Tambourine and
Dancer with Castanets
Oil on canvas; each 61" × 25 1/2".
Signed and dated: "Renoir 09."
Acquired from Philippe Cangnat in 1961.

and compactness of the figures, which are as simplified and reduced to essentials as Cycladic idols. They are gripped in the powerful framework made by the violent color and intense light of their "natural" setting. Cézanne went over the work again and again, creating a thick crust of paint; nevertheless, every brushstroke is essential. This is one of the most "abstract" of Cézanne's paintings. Severe yet sensual, it epitomizes the simple solidity of the female bodies and the burning color of the Mediterranean light. It combines the wild romanticism and the patient research in composition and color that coexist in all of the artist's work.

AUGUSTE RENOIR.   *Dancer With Tambourine* and *Dancer With Castanets*.   p. 142

Typical of the artist's late works, these two canvases were painted in the summer of 1909 for Maurice Cangnat's dining room in Paris. They were placed at the sides of a mantelpiece surmounted by a large antique mirror, as though they were caryatids. The head of the *Dancer With Castanets* is a portrait of Renoir's favorite model, Gabrielle Renard, who was the cousin and nurse of his son Jean. The model for the two bodies and the face of the *Dancer With Tambourine* was Mme. Georgette Pigeot, a dressmaker and friend of the family. Renoir's joy in life and color is fully expressed here, unhampered by the crippling infirmity of his hands at this period of his life.

SPAIN

EL GRECO. *Christ Driving the Traders from the Temple.*

The inventory of the artist's goods compiled after his death lists four versions of this subject. Numerous replicas, variants and copies also attest to the popularity of the composition. An earlier version, painted before El Greco's arrival in Toledo in 1577, includes portraits of Michelangelo, Titian and Raphael. Michelangelo and Tintoretto inspired the poses of

144

EL GRECO
(DOMENICO THEOTOKOPOULOS)
Crete 1541 — Toledo 1614
Christ Driving the Traders from the Temple
Oil on canvas; 41 3/4" × 51".
A few more inches of painted canvas are folded back on the stretcher.
Sir J. C. Robinson presented the painting to the Gallery in 1895.

almost all the figures in the painting. The perspective of the background recalls Palladio and Veronese, and the organization of the whole composition shows an assimilation of Italian High Renaissance devices. The spiraling torsion of the figure of Christ starts the agitated gesticulating movement, which turns on an axis placed left of center. The groups are set into a radiating fan-shaped system of movements. But the architectonic solidity of the Italian tradition is transformed by the flickering of El Greco's light and color. This new insubstantial character creates the excitement and visionary aspect of his work.

On pages 146–147:
DIEGO VELÁZQUEZ
Seville 1599 — Madrid 1660
The Toilet of Venus ("The Rokeby Venus")
Oil on canvas; 48 1/4″ × 69 3/4″.
Considerable repainting has been done, some of which covers the cuts made by a suffragette in 1914. In 1651 it belonged to Don Gaspar Méndez de Haro, Marqués del Carpio, who may have commissioned it. Acquired by the Gallery from Thomas Agnew in 1906.

DIEGO VELÁZQUEZ. *The Toilet of Venus ("The Rokeby Venus").*

pp. 146–147

Although the painting of nudes was not encouraged in Counter-Reformation Spain, Velázquez did at least four other such pictures that have not survived. Critics debate whether this work was painted before, during or after the artist's second visit to Italy in 1648–51. The influences he acquired at that time do not necessarily have a bearing on the painting since, apart from the theme and the presence of the winged cupid, it is not derived from classical idealism. It shows instead a spontaneous participation in human life and experience, with no sacred or scholarly references. The point of view is detached and meticulously observant. In composition, the curve of the slim youthful body is echoed in the bed clothes and the curtain. These movements are countered by the figure of the cupid and by the mirror which reflects the secret image of Venus' face. Color and tone subtly record every change in contour and texture, creating a sensitively vibrant picture.

DIEGO VELÁZQUEZ. *Philip IV of Spain in Brown and Silver. p. 148*
The similarity in pose of this painting to the portrait Rubens painted during his embassy to Spain (now in the Durazzo Giustiniani collection in Genoa) suggests that Velázquez did his version after his first visit to Italy in 1629. Evidently Velázquez, who attached enough importance to his portrait to have signed it, worked on it for several years after his return to Spain. One of the work's purposes, in fact, must have been to serve as a prototype for numerous copies made for official distribution. With his elaborately embroidered suit, the King is wearing a gold chain with the Order of the

DIEGO VELÁZQUEZ
Philip IV of Spain in Brown and Silver
Oil on canvas; 6'4 3/4" × 3'7 1/4".
Signed on the paper in the subject's right
hand: *Señor. / Diego Velsquz. / Pintor de
V.Mg.* (Sir: Diego Velazquez, Your Majesty's Painter). The painting was confiscated
by Joseph Bonaparte. The Gallery acquired
it in 1882 at the sale of the Hamilton collection.

Golden Arrow. The upstanding collar became fashionable at the Spanish
court after 1623. The color range is sober and simple, but the embroidered
suit is like an explosion of sparks. An arbitrary shadow behind the head
brings out the King's golden hair and pink face.

FRANCISCO DE ZURBARÁN
Fuentes de Cantos (Badajoz) 1598 —
Madrid 1664
St. Francis in Meditation
Oil on canvas; 63 3/4″ × 54″.
Signed on the paper at lower right; "Fran.co
Dezurbara / faciebat / 1639." It belonged to
Sir Arthur Ashton in the mid-nineteenth cen-
tury, and came to the Gallery in 1964 with
the Major C. E. W. Wood Bequest.

FRANCISCO DE ZURBARÁN.   *St. Francis in Meditation.*

Zurbarán often did single-figure compositions such as this one, since they showed to best advantage his stripped-down forms, which are among the most elemental in seventeenth-century Spanish painting. He was a follower of Caravaggio in his feeling for form as well as in the dramatic single-source lighting which defines his volumes. The main compositional movement is the diagonal that divides the picture and is supported on the right by the cubic form on which the figure is leaning. All the other elements are adroitly set at angles that either check or reinforce this movement. Although the subject is religious, Zurbarán did not stress psychological or mystical allusions. A major interest of the work is its compact construction of lighted and shadowed planes, which throw the figure into monumental relief.

FRANCISCO GOYA.   *Dr. Peral.*   *p. 150*

In this painting, one of the major works of the last phase of Goya's career, all extraneous detail has been stripped away. The figure of Dr. Peral — the financial representative of the Spanish government in Paris in the late eighteenth century — is set at an angle and posed so that it forms a pyramid around its own axis. Seated on the edge of the shadow, it is caught by a diffused light that slides along the surfaces and is reflected in highlights on

149

the face and in the sheen of the silk. Light, flying brushstrokes trace the range of clear colors. Only the tormented and bitter face shows some of the drama and melancholy of Goya's expressive art.

FRANCISCO GOYA. *Doña Isabel Cobos de Porcel.*
This work is usually dated 1806, as this is the year inscribed on the portrait of the subject's husband, Don Antonio Porcel (now in the Jockey Club, Buenos Aires). But that painting is not a companion to this one, and was probably executed a few years earlier. The blond Castilian is dressed in the folk costume of the *Maja,* and has been posed in a self-assured way that emphasizes her imperious beauty. The composition is a rhomboid, diag-

FRANCISCO GOYA
Fuendetodos 1746 — Bordeaux 1828
Dr. Peral
Oil on poplar panel; 37 1/2″ × 25 3/4″.
The painting belonged to the heirs of the subject until the end of the nineteenth century. It was presented to the National Gallery by Sir G. Donaldson in 1904.

onally divided by the black lace mantilla. Beneath the lace are seen the fiery glints of her red silk dress. In this celebration of surging vitality, Goya harks back to Titian and Velázquez for his expressive means. This portrait belongs with the series of queenly figures in modern Western art that represent the Romantic idea of the "eternally feminine."

FRANCISCO GOYA.   *A Scene from "The Forcibly Bewitched"*
                            (*El Hechizado por Fuerza*).   *p. 152*

There are numerous instances of the witchcraft theme in the body of Goya's work. Here it appears in one of the five pictures Goya painted for the Duke of Osuna's country house, the Alameda. The scene, taken from the second

act of Zamora's play, *The Forcibly Bewitched*, shows the timorous Don Claudio, who is convinced that he has been bewitched, as he fills the oil lamp. He believes that he will die if it goes out. Goya often painted pictures revealing the obscurantism that afflicts people, the savagery of man, and the human shackles of dreams, superstition and fear. Here he creates dramatic effect out of the black silhouette of the priest, the greenish goat-devil and the looming figures of the malignant dancing donkeys.

FRANCISCO GOYA
A Scene from "The Forcibly Bewitched"
(El Hechizado por Fuerza)
Oil on canvas; 16 3/4" × 12".
The comedy, *The Forcibly Bewitched,* was written by Antonio de Zamora, and was first performed in 1698.
Painted for the Duke of Osuna around 1798, the canvas was bought by the National Gallery at the sale of the collection in Madrid, 1896.

ENGLAND

WILLIAM HOGARTH. *The Shrimp Girl.*

A central figure in English art, Hogarth is best known for his moralizing and satirical outlook. With a mass public for his engravings, he was also in demand as a portrait painter of the prosperous middle class. He was Court Painter and a supporter of Parliament's program to reform morals. Hogarth was self-taught, at first following the examples of Jan Steen and Flemish genre painting, then looking toward such diverse painters as Rubens, Chardin and Rembrandt. This portrait is exceptionally impressive and immediate in its effect. The broad brushwork looks as if it had just been laid down and the paint appears still wet. The elementary strength of Hogarth's range of greens and reds emphasizes the vigor of a style in which the simplicity achieved is a mature interpretation of imagination.

SIR JOSHUA REYNOLDS. *Lady Cockburn and Her Three Eldest Sons.* *p. 156*

First president and leading spirit of the Royal Academy, which was founded by George III in 1768, Reynolds was at the center of the English art world. For him, art was both a profession and a cultural product; as the latter, it derived mainly from the classical tradition of Raphael, Correggio and van Dyck. Official portrait painter to English high society, Reynolds raised his subjects to the heaven of mythology and history. In composition, this painting derives from the Italian allegory of *Charity:* the children are more like cupids in the mythological tradition than individualized figures, just as the mother is closer to the idea of the Roman matron than to that of an English lady. The broad facing of the dark mantle forms the base of a pyramidal structure, which narrows above with the three little children who seem to revolve around their mother. In a subtle rhythm, they embody one of the canons of classicism that Reynolds expressed with such mastery.

THOMAS GAINSBOROUGH. *Mrs. Siddons.* *p. 156*

This is one of the artist's most famous portraits, in which his vision of the world appears in its most sumptuous form. The figure of the actress is pervaded with nervous, flashing tremors and vibrations — from the curls to the muff, from the blue stripes of the dress and the white ribbon on the right arm to the flaming background. The brushwork is a pictorial play of transparencies, lights, colors and contrasts, expressing a mobile sensitivity that dissolves the formality of the pose. The novelty of this expressive means is apparent when compared to a portrait of the same subject by Gainsborough's contemporary, Reynolds. There she is allegorized as the Tragic Muse, in a composition resounding with rather self-satisfied reminiscences of Michelangelo.

WILLIAM HOGARTH
London 1697 — London 1764
The Shrimp Girl
Oil on canvas; 25″ × 20 3/4″.
Probably executed as the model for an engraving around 1740, it was inherited by Mary Lewis from the artist's widow. Bought by the National Gallery at the Sir Philip Miles sale.

THOMAS GAINSBOROUGH. *The Morning Walk: William Hallett and His Wife Elizabeth.*

A nuptial portrait that has always been very popular, this is one of the few in which newlyweds are shown together. The figures are set in natural surroundings that are not stated with the force and independence of Romantic art. The background is made of the same rhythms, the same changing transparencies as the figures — especially the woman. This is a scene reconstructed from memory in the artist's studio. It is one of Gainsborough's last works, when his quick sensitivity was apt to fall into repetitious formulas.

THOMAS GAINSBOROUGH. *The Painter's Daughters Teasing a Cat.* p. 158

Like the other double portrait in the National Gallery, this unfinished work portrays Mary and Margaret Gainsborough, and was probably begun after the artist's second move with his family from Ipswich to Bath, the fashionable watering place. Only the splendidly executed heads are finished, while the rest is sketched in rapid strokes on an ocher ground which

Above, right:
THOMAS GAINSBOROUGH
Sudbury (Suffolk) 1727 — London 1788
Mrs. Siddons (1783–85)
Oil on canvas; 49 1/4" × 39 1/4".
Shown at the Manchester exhibition of 1857.
Bought for the National Gallery in 1862.

Above, left:
SIR JOSHUA REYNOLDS
Plympton Earl 1723 — London 1792
Lady Cockburn and Her Three Eldest Sons
Oil on canvas; 55 3/4" × 44 1/2".
Signed: 1773/J. Reynolds: Pinx.
The engraving made from this painting eighteen years later, on the request of the subject's husband, Sir James Cockburn, was entitled *Cornelia and Her Sons.*
Bequeathed by Alfred Beit, 1906.

Right:
THOMAS GAINSBOROUGH
The Morning Walk: William Hallett and His Wife Elizabeth
Oil on canvas; 7'8" × 5'10".
William Hallett married Elizabeth Stephen in July 1785, and the portrait was probably completed by the autumn of the same year.
Acquired from Lord Rothschild in 1954.

156

provides a transparent underpainting. The two figures are set in an oval described by the arm of the elder sister. This movement is taken up below by the younger sister's arm, the cat and the sleeve, and is repeated in the yellow sky of the background. If we compare this portrait with a much larger one painted almost ten years later (now in the Whitbread collection), its fervent warmth becomes strikingly clear in contrast to the conventionality of the other, in which the sumptuous dresses are mere tinsel covering two conventionally posed mannequins.

JOHN CONSTABLE.   *Weymouth Bay.*

Constable's sketches, rather than the pictures he exhibited at the Royal Academy, reveal the quality and novelty of his art. In this work we see how the artist gave the landscape a particular character simply by his manner of representing it. The light is the dominant element that builds up and brings out the forms, and turns a bleak bay into a monumental landscape. The sky is not an empty background but a weighty protagonist in the scene, as are the earth and sea over which it looms. Effects of light are rendered by direct, adroit use of the palette knife.

159

JOSEPH MALLORD WILLIAM TURNER. *Sun Rising Through Vapor: Fishermen Cleaning and Selling Fish.*

Considered the founder of Romantic landscape painting, Turner saw his subjects primarily in terms of the light absorbing forms and transforming them into chromatic vibrations. Turner revolutionized the English and Flemish tradition of highly defined and detailed landscape; especially after his stay in Venice, he replaced the topographical view with a single blaze of space and light. In this early painting, he blended sea and sky into a single luminous entity that radiates reflections eliptically, lighting up the human figures seen against the dark silhouette of the boats.

160

JOSEPH MALLORD WILLIAM TURNER
London 1775 — London 1851
Sun Rising Through Vapor:
Fisherman Cleaning and Selling Fish (1807)
Oil on canvas; 53″ × 70 1/2″.
Exhibited at the Royal Academy in 1807 and at the British Institution in 1809. In 1810 it was offered to Sir John Fleming Leicester but, according to Turner's own opinion, it needed cleaning. This suggests that it was not a very recent work, even though the experimental methods used by the artist often quickly altered the original appearance of his paintings. Acquired by Leicester (later Lord De Tabley) in 1818, and reacquired by the artist in 1827. Part of the Turner Bequest to the National Gallery, 1856.

HISTORY OF THE MUSEUM
AND ITS BUILDING

HISTORY OF THE COLLECTIONS

The National Gallery of London houses one of the world's most notable collections of European painting. Unlike other national galleries that began as royal collections, this gallery from its beginning has had to select its acquisitions most rigorously, since its funds were supplied by the British government. It is thus one of the earliest examples of a gallery conceived and managed as a public service, an example followed by many American museums.

The Gallery was created out of the enthusiasm of several English collectors and the generosity of others. Parliament authorized the formation of a museum in 1824, and purchased thirty-eight works from the collection of John Julius Angerstein, a merchant who had died the year before. In all, the sum of £60,000 was allocated for acquisitions and running expenses. This first purchase included the six paintings of Hogarth's series, *Marriage à la Mode,* and five canvases by Claude Lorraine. A little more than a month later, the gallery was officially opened in the Angerstein house at 100 Pall Mall. New works were soon acquired, including Correggio's *Madonna of the Basket* and Titian's *Bacchus and Ariadne,* as well as the sixteen paintings of the Beaumont collection, the most notable of which were Rubens' *Castle of Steen* and Canaletto's *Venice: Campo S. Vidal and S. Maria della Carità.* With the addition of the Rev. William Holwell Carr Bequest in 1831, the collection had outgrown its quarters. The six directors commissioned the imposing building by the architect William Wilkins, facing Trafalgar Square, which was completed in 1838.

The Gallery's move to the new building coincided with the advent of the Victorian Age, which was marked by a growing public interest in the cultural facilities of the capital. A period of intensive development began, and acquisitions were made frequently and regularly with funds from Parliament. At first the collection consisted mainly of works representing the various Continental schools of painting; around mid-century, however, the gallery began to acquire English paintings, including Robert Vernon's donation in 1847 of 157 English and modern pictures and Turner's bequest in 1856 of 105 of his own drawings, watercolors and oil paintings. Many of these were among the 130 works that were transferred from the National Gallery to the Tate Gallery, which was opened in 1897.

By 1855 the National Gallery had become a major institution. Its administration was revamped to consist of a Board of Management headed by a director. The first director was the painter and connoisseur Sir Charles Eastlake, who in his ten years as director enlarged the collection to include even unfashionable artists. Under his directorship the Gallery acquired such works as Paolo Uccello's *Niccolò da Tolentino at the Battle of San Romano*, Piero della Francesca's *The Baptism of Christ*, the fragment of Rogier van der Weyden's *The Magdalen Read-*

ing, Botticelli's *Portrait of a Young Man* and Bronzino's *An Allegory of Time and Love* — paintings still considered among the major treasures of the collection. In the same period Queen Victoria donated a number of German paintings to the Gallery in memory of Prince Albert.

During the last thirty years of the nineteenth century the National Gallery acquired some of its most notable works. These included, in 1871, paintings by Rubens and other Flemish and Dutch masters from the Sir Robert Peel collection, and in 1876 the ninety-four pictures from the Wynn Ellis collection. In 1885 Raphael's *The Ansidei Madonna* and van Dyck's *Charles I on Horseback* came to the Gallery, in 1892 Vermeer's *A Young Woman Seated at a Virginal,* and in 1899 the two Rembrandts from Lord Saumarez' collection. An example of the munificence of private citizens who continued to support the National Gallery was the acquisition in 1890 of three paintings from Longford Castle: Holbein's *The Ambassadors,* Veláquez' *Portrait of Admiral Pulido-Pareja* and Moroni's *A Nobleman.* This purchase was made possible by the contribution of £ 10,000 each by Lord Rothschild, Lord Iveagh and Charles Cotes. In 1849 the Board of Management acquired responsibility with the director for the choice of acquisitions. In 1903 a special fund was set up for purchasing new works. A year later Titian's famous *Portrait of a Man* was acquired from the Darnley collection, and in 1909 Holbein's *Christina of Denmark, Duchess of Milan* was bought

through the fund. Other acquisitions around that time included a Frans

Hals in 1908, the Masaccio in 1916, and nineteenth-century French paintings in 1918. At the same time the collection was considerably enriched by such bequests as that of George Salting in 1910, who left it 192 pictures, including the Master of Flémalle's *The Virgin and Child before a Firescreen*. In 1915, Hugh Lane bequeathed his nineteenth-century French paintings, including Renoir's *The Umbrellas* ("*Les Parapluies*"), and in 1924 Dr. Ludwig Mond left the Gallery his *Crucifixion* by Raphael and Titian's *Madonna and Child*.

During World War II the National Gallery was badly damaged by bombs. An entire room was destroyed and others in the east wing were ruined. In recent years, after rebuilding and reorganizing the lighting and exhibition of the works, an air-conditioning system was installed. Meanwhile the collection has continued to grow, and recent notable acquisitions include El Greco's *The Adoration of the Name of Jesus*, Rogier van der Weyden's *Pietà*, Memling's *Donne Triptych*, Rembrandt's *Portrait of an Old Man Seated*, Poussin's *The Adoration of the Shepherds*, Jordaens' *Double Portrait*, Gainsborough's *Mr. and Mrs. Robert Andrews*, Leonardo's cartoon of *St. Anne* and Paolo Uccello's *St. George and the Dragon*.

The National Gallery has its own photographic service, publishes catalogs and annuals, periodically puts on exhibitions, and has a laboratory for restoring and conserving pictures.

THE BUILDING

The National Gallery's building is not commonly considered one of William Wilkins' most felicitous architectural achievements. Erected between 1832 and 1838 at Trafalgar Square, it was intended to blend into John Nash's town-planning scheme for the visual linking of some of the key points in central London. Wilkins designed a long Academic façade, using some of the elegant forty-year-old Corinthian columns from Carlton House, and crowning the building with a small dome of Byzantine inspiration. The interior has been considerably altered over the years. In 1876 E. M. Barry designed a new wing for the Vernon collection, and in 1885–87 the central stairs and the vestibules were added. Today the Gallery is laid out in a sequence of national divisions by schools of painting.

LEGEND

	Room
Bellini and Giorgione	IX
England — 18th & 19th centuries	XVI
Domenichino	XIIIA
Holland — 17th century	X, XI, XII, XV
Flanders — 17th century	XIV, XV
France — 17th century	XVIIB, XXII
France — 18th century	XIX
France — 19th century	XXI, XXII, XXIII
Germany	VIIIA
Leonardo's Cartoon	V
Italy — 14th century	I, II
Italy — 15th century (Florence, Central Italy)	III, IV, VIIIC
Italy — 15th & early 16th centuries (Milan)	IIA
Italy — 15th century (North, Venice)	VIIIB, XIIIC
Italy — 16th century	VI
Italy — 16th century (North)	XIII
Italy — 16th century (Venice)	VII
Italy — 17th century	XVIIA, XVIIB, XVIIC
Italy — 18th century	XIIIB, XVII, XVIID
Netherlands — 15th & 16th centuries	XVIII, VIIID
Spain	XVIII
Wilton Diptych	II

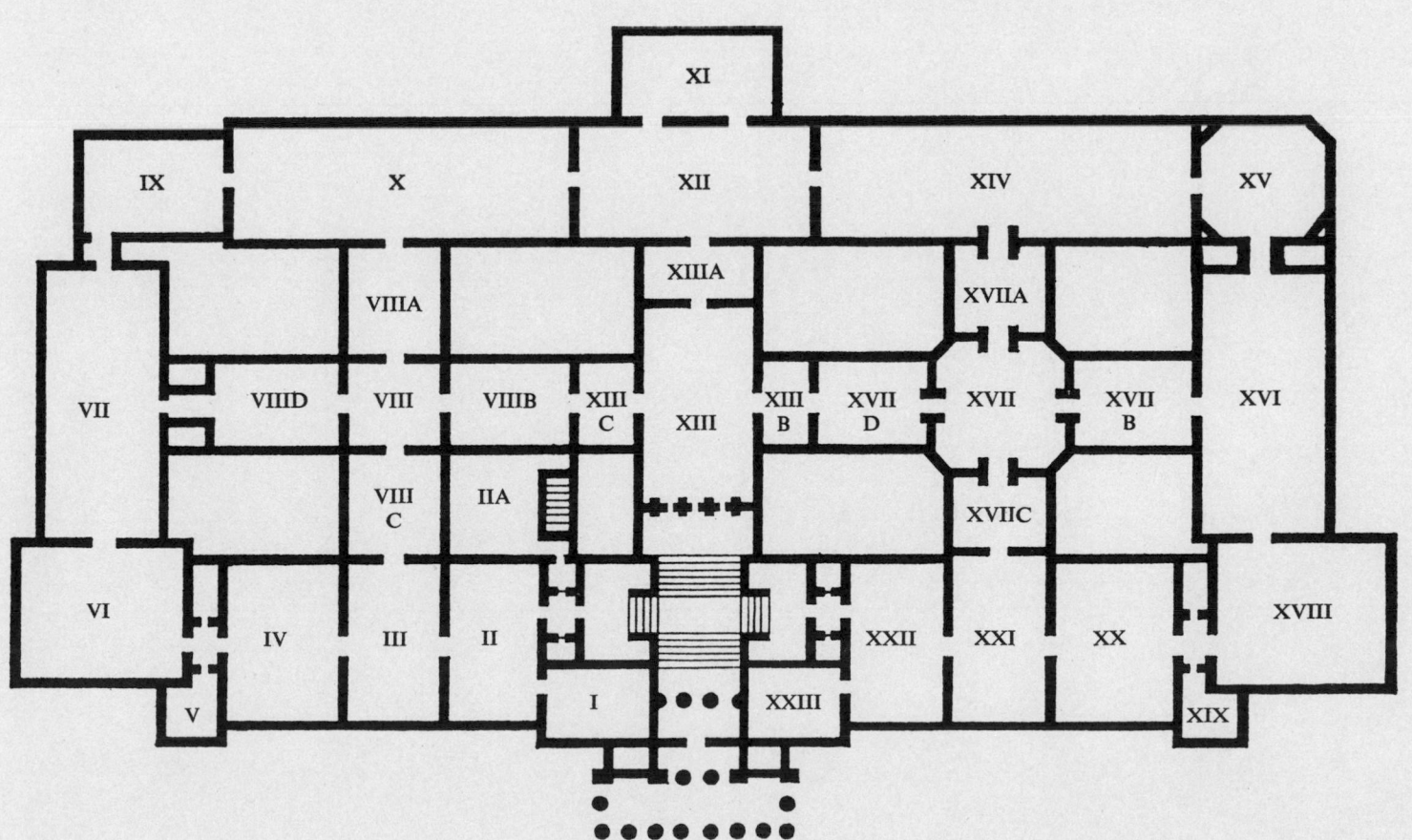

167

SELECTED BIBLIOGRAPHY

BENESCH, OTTO. *German Painting: From Dürer to Holbein.* (World Publishing Co., Geneva, 1966).

BERENSON, BERNARD. *Italian Painters of the Renaissance.* (Phaidon, London, 1953).

DUPONT, J. and MATHEY, F. *The Seventeenth Century: From Caravaggio to Vermeer.* (Skira, Geneva, 1951).

FLETCHER, JENNIFER. *Peter Paul Rubens.* (Phaidon, London, 1968).

FORMAGGIO, DINO. *Goya.* (Thomas Yoseloff, New York, 1961).

FROMENTIN, EUGENE. *The Masks of Past Time: Dutch and Flemish Painting from Van Eyck to Rembrandt.* tr. by A. Boyle. (Phaidon, London, 1948).

HENDY, PHILIP. *The National Gallery, London.* (Harry N. Abrams, Inc., New York, 1960).

MUNZ, LUDWIG. *Rembrandt.* (Abrams, New York, 1954).

ROTHENSTEIN, JOHN and BUTLIN, MARTIN. *Turner.* (George Braziller, New York, 1964).

SCHNEIDER, BRUNO F. *Renoir.* (Crown Publishers, New York, 1958).

VALSECCHI, MARCO. *National Gallery, London.* (Appleton-Century, New York, 1965).

INDEX OF ILLUSTRATIONS

INDEX OF NAMES

GENERAL INDEX